Mutton's Decadence

"The Last Prophet"
Malachi 4:5

Elijah

BY:

Mickey R. Mullen

FolioAvenue Publishing Service
2031 Union Street, Suite 6,
San Francisco CA 94123
415-869-8834 (866-365-4628)
www.folioavenue.com

ISBN (Paperback): 978-1-951193-78-2

DEDICATION

I would like to dedicate this novel to the following individuals. Without their love, this venture would have never come to be.

God — I never knew that I was Elijah, the prophet of Malachi 4:5, growing up. He kept me alive too many times to ignore. A head-on collision in a car, attempted suicide, another car wreck in a snowstorm stopping three feet short of an eighteen-wheeler at five below zero, no stranger to guns, knives, police, and irate husbands, I just hope I can be the servant that God wants me to be.

Mom — with me putting every gray hair on her head, she gave me unconditional love its definition but never said the word *love.*

Dad — Mike Mullen, a Protestant minister in my childhood days, who took me to church. It had a bearing on the outcome when I was seeking salvation at the age of thirty-one.

Marguerite — my sister, with her sense of humor, makes life almost worth living.

Paul — my brother who was the farmer and had in feeding the family, sacrificing his own childhood from the time he could walk, and a VFW (veteran of three foreign women).

TABLE OF CONTENT

ACKNOWLEDGMENTS

I really must acknowledge two people here. Without their hard work and dedication to the project, you, my reader, would not be holding this volume in your hands. Hope Edwards — the editor of the book that left it the way the author wrote it, in a fast-paced autobiography that is not in sequential order just like the KJ Bible of 1611.

Kevin — I don't know what I would have done without him and his knowledge, from typography to formatting, book cover creation to publication in various channels. Kevin was a godsend.

INTRODUCTION

Most people would call our family dysfunctional. As a baby, did I have a choice in the matter? Whatever, I don't think I got far off the track.

Not long after being born, I became a PK (Preacher's Kid), and in some churches, that automatically puts a child in the kingdom of heaven. The preacher said it was sacrilegious for anyone to pray without seeking salvation. The Sunday school teacher asked me one time to dismiss the class; I never said a word, and my dad was the ordained minister. If she said anything to him, I took a chance on Dad's wrath or going to hell. I chose his wrath.

I never saw anything in the church at that time that I wanted. When a person sat on the back row of the church, smelling of tobacco smoke, it intrigued me. At times, I did feel the convictive spirit of being a sinner but never went to the altar at that time.

In this book, you will find out why I swore to never let myself fall in love. Knowing normal when I see it, I rejected it. Without the interference of love, I led more of a spontaneous existence of free will, moving by a natural feeling of impulse without constraint, effort, or forethought. It did not conform to society. Having lived the church way of life until the age of nine, it was hard to go back to it, but I did at the age of thirty-one. I know it will be hard to understand, but the sins or decadence that I committed, God forgave, and that is all one needs in this life. The way that I have to lived might have something to do with the fact that as a child my upbringing was in

1

religious Protestant environment, and at the time, I didn't believe what my dad was preaching. At the age of thirty-one, that proved to be correct. When I was nine, my dad got into an argument in a Sunday school class in Rapid City, South Dakota, and the family quit going to church.

Mom filed for a divorce in Rapid City, and Dad became an alcoholic. At fifteen, I started drinking in the bars, and at that time, you only had to be eighteen. However, I found out that all you needed was the price of the drink in what we called the 3.2 beer bars where most of the Sioux Indians drank.

The book goes from when we were building a house, after I was born, and living in a homemade trailer to at nineteen, going through the windshield of a car. Eight years in the US Navy, thirteen years as a union carpenter, and taking care of Mom in her home before she had to go to a nursing home. One chapter is about religion and salvation, the way that I experienced it. I know of no church or religious organization's doctrine that compares with it.

Which church or religious organization has the way to the kingdom of heaven? As it reads in St. John 3:4, "How can a man be born when he is old? Can he enter into his mother's womb, and be born?" When you see the kingdom of God, a person sees the power of God. This was after Jesus told Nicodemus that a man must be born again, in St. John 3:5, "Jesus answered, Verily, verily, I say unto thee, Except a man be born of water" (a parable that means born again in the third verse) "and of the Spirit" (Holy Ghost), "he cannot enter into the kingdom of God."

Chapter 1

PUSHED INTO THE WORLD

About 8:00 a.m. on September 20, 1937, I took my first breath. The midwife that delivered me never put blanket over me, as her main profession was calves. When Mike (Dad) came in the house, he noticed the discrepancy and mentioned it to the midwife, but it was too late, the damage was done, with an ear infection that the doctor lanced. Paul told me the cow blew bran in my face because I was born inside a stockyard, in the caretaker's house, in Laramie, Wyoming with freckles on my face.

On that day, there was a snowstorm raging, and today, it is 85 degrees. My mother (Ida) had polio when she was three years old and that caused her left leg to be in a weakened condition.

Her mother passed away when she was in the tenth grade of high school, and she inherited her job of janitor and a small house. The house they traded for a milk cow, after my brother (Paul) was born. Mom was a Baptist but attended the Assembly of God Church, when Dad received a certificate of an ordained minister.

One of his sisters introduced my mother to Dad, and they married. Later I learned, after my parents were married, Dad hopped on a train and left town.

In those days, such men we called hobos, and several times, he mentioned a hobo killed on some train while traveling around the country. I have wondered at times if he had anything to do with it.

Was Dad capable of murder? My sister (Sis or Marguerita) and I believed so. A TV show said the murder of a hobo was commonplace even if they had on a good pair of shoes. Life must have never meant much during that time. One such story I heard said a carpenter apprentice working with Dad died in Milwaukee, Wisconsin, under questionable circumstances, falling off a high-rise building. More than once, he told me he never liked to work with an apprentice.

When Dad came back, he built a trailer on a truck frame, out of two-by-fours sawed in half. Paul told me he lived in the trailer for five years. The reason that he built it was to pull it into Kansas to follow the yearly wheat harvest. He had a couple of problems though. The first was pulling it with the old cars that he owned. The other was the grasshoppers liked the linseed oil that he put on the canvas for weatherproofing and they chewed holes in it. Sometimes, Paul had to get out on some of the hills and put a brick behind the wheel, as Dad popped (released) the clutch to inch the car forward. At least once, he got his fingers between the brick and the tire.

Sis was born while they lived in the trailer in Laramie, Wyoming, by the same midwife. The homemade trailer house was probably not more that sixteen feet long and eight feet wide. Built on a truck frame, it allowed that total square footage. Sis was five years older than I was, and Paul was seven years older.

The last time they pulled the trailer from Kansas to Laramie, Wyoming, Mom was pregnant with me, and when

I was about due for delivery, she went to caretaker's house inside the stockyards. The same morning, Dad went to the railroad yard and asked them for a job. They told him to report for work the next morning. It was the first good job that he had ever had. He was lucky in the fact that when World War II came about, he deferred from going into the army.

Chapter 2

NEW HOUSE IN LARAMIE

Dad went to a lumberyard in Laramie, Wyoming, and asked the manager if he could buy materials on credit to build a house. He gave him permission, and he bought the lot where the trailer was located. The family used as outhouse, as they were called, "a wooden structure built over a hole," for a bathroom.

With a pick, shovel, wheelbarrow, and Paul's little red wagon, the family begin digging out the basement. By today's standards, in most places, it would be against the law to live on the same lot. The government wants you to live in a swank motel while you dig out the basement by hand. With the basement dug out, next came the footing for the walls, if there were any.

When the concrete walls were poured using a wheelbarrow, he had the tendency to put more rocks in the walls that concrete, as they were cheaper. They made the concrete for the footing and walls on the building site, and the house is still there today. Next came the main wood floor that he weatherproofed by putting black felt paper over it.

We moved into the basement, and we had to follow the potbellied stove for heat. It was a move up.

To go down into the basement, he built a stairway, covered with a door, next to the left front corner of the house. Dad always wanted the family working with him.

I'm not sure what Mom did with me; I was probably put in a chest of drawer so she could help.

Paul was seven years old at the time and was his main man. He had migraine headaches at times, and Dad told me years later that the reason he spanked him so often was he thought he was trying to get out of work. Paul had a case of appendicitis that broke and somehow, he got over it. He told me when he went home from the hospital that there was a tube that drained the poison out of his body.

Because Dad worked on the railroad, he asked the man that shoveled coal in the boiler of the train if he could drop off a little coal at Cedar Street, and Paul walked down the tracks with his red wagon to pick it up. The coal was for the potbellied stove and cook stove in the trailer.

Sis was no stranger to his wrath and Mom also, if she made him mad. He would tell her "If you were a man," and slam a door more than once, either on the car or house.

Working on the railroad and building the house was no easy task, but he started building the main house as soon as he could. One of the men he worked with said he had a dog, if he wanted it. Rex came home with him, and if he ever got good meal in his lifetime, I'm not sure when it was. Rex was part pit bull, and I never saw him lose a fight.

At that time, a lot of stray dogs roamed around, and a lot of dogfights took place. With all the noise going on, the dog and I tried to run away from home more than once, as soon as I could walk. Adoption was not far from my mind, if they would take both of us.

Paul said Dad guessed at the slope of the roof, and today, it shows. The roof construction is something that you wouldn't find in any builder's manual. Sis said it had a small bathroom, kitchen, and one bedroom. The only thing that I remember was a couch and the potbellied stove in the front room.

With the house sort of finished, there was a sewer ditch at the front of the house. At the time, I must have been three or four years old. Dad and Mom were having sex on the couch on the front room. I was playing with my few toys on the floor in the front of the couch. When Dad was through in a couple of minutes, he stepped over me with one leg and that left his genitals above me, and I was impressed.

The next day, I was in the sewer ditch with my friend next door, and I had his penis out of his pants. His wasn't any bigger than what I had; we were both shortchanged. Looking up on the bank, there was Mom looking down at me. She said, "Get in the house. I'm going to tell your dad when he gets home from work."

When the wrath of God showed up, he went outside to a tree, cut off several branches, and came back inside. Near the potbellied stove, he proceeded to beat me from my knees to my waist.

He came at me twice, and I couldn't get my breath the first time through the second beating. I'm not sure how long a person can live without breathing. Between the tears and not breathing, Dad asked me if I wanted some more "If you don't stop crying." It wasn't long into the beating that Mom was screaming for him to stop. Just today, I heard of a child having a seizure from holding their breath too long in a normal crying situation, and they had to go to the hospital. The beating left scars on my body, from my waist to my knees.

When Mom was older, I asked her if she remembered Dad beating me. She said "Dad never laid a hand on you in his entire life." I never ask her where the scars came from.

Not long afterward, he said he was called to preach, and in the Bible, it says, "Not to spare the rod." He quit his deferred job from going into World War II and sold the house. He drove the Model A Ford to Seneca, Missouri, and bought a house; it was more of a rocky hill than anything a person could farm. At that time, all he thought about was a house to live in, and that was about all that was there. He was going to live on his preacher's salary. After buying the house, he drove the car over to the train station to leave it there and probably either hitchhiked or rode back to Laramie on freight trains. The family rode back to Seneca on a passenger train and Sis remembered two nuns dressed in their habits. I remembered a man making a hat for me out of a newspaper. Neither one of us remembered Paul being on the train, but he must have been.

Chapter 3

FARM IN SENECA, MISSOURI

We had moved to the farm in the autumn of 1941 or '42, when nothing would grow in a garden. The first three or four months, pinto beans and cornbread were all I remembered eating most of the time. Paul, with his .22 rifle, shot a rabbit or squirrel, and we ate bullfrog legs. He found wild honey at times in trees and would get it. Molasses and honey were used for a sweetener because sugar was one of the items that was rationed during World War II. Gasoline for the car was another item that was rationed by the government. To hunt the squirrels, I would walk a short distance in front of Paul to get the squirrel to go around the tree so he could shoot it. In the spring, seed potatoes were on the menu. The differences were they had sprouts growing out of them, and they would become soft. I have a VCR tape where Dad said, "We ate the same bran that he fed the horses." It was the first time that I ever heard that statement.

They heated water on the cookstove for our Saturday night baths, and it used coal. Because I was the smallest, I got in the galvanized tub first, then Sis. Each time, hot water was added to the tub when another person took their bath. Dad and Mom was last; we had to look good for church on Sunday. We used a potbellied stove for heat, and Mom usually had the job of starting a fire in the morning.

When we went to bed, Mom would heat bricks, roll it up in a newspaper for the kids, and the parent used a hot water bottles to knock the chill. Can you imagine how cold it would be in the morning before a fire was started? For

10

drinking water, there was a pump over a well out in the yard. It was a death sentence to use up all the water to prime the pump.

We hadn't lived in Seneca very long, and Dad received a letter in the mail to report to the army recruiter. He hotfooted it to Kansas City, Missouri; ran into a boss that he knew from Laramie; and was hired back in the railroad. Paul told me he was transferred to Kansas City, but how often do they transfer a man that specializes in grease? I was there when he got the letter and read it to Mom.

He never had time to get established in a church before he left. With Dad in Kansas City, that left the family fending for themselves. Paul was only eleven or twelve, and he did most of the farmwork with the horses: Dick, Duke, and Prince. In the spring, we had a large garden, and Dad would drive from Kansas City on the weekends. Mom was hoeing the weeds, so Dad hooked up the plow to the horse to show her how to hoe the weeds. We ate what was left after the horse trampled the good vines. It was the last time he ever did that.

Mom went to Joplin, Missouri, and had a hysterectomy shortly after we arrived in Seneca. Sis said she showed her the bloody bandage and almost fainted. Sis taught me a little tune on the piano when she came home. I wouldn't have a little brother or sister to play with.

On one of the trips to Kansas City, Dad said two motorcycles crowded him off the road. The Model A Ford rolled over and ended up on its wheels. He said his Bible was on the seat, and he preached a sermon for those that stopped. The Model A Ford started, and he went on down the road.

He went to a lumberyard and bought a window for a house for a windshield. He built a top out canvas and put linseed oil on it for a preservative. The Ford he rolled was a convertible, so he put the plastic that was in the back window in the side doors.

Mom cut her arm with a knife, and she told Sis to go to the farm next door and get Lloyd Keith. He came riding up on spirited horse that I had never seen before. It would make Roy Roger's Trigger look like a Shetland pony. I believed that was when the affair started. I wish I could say that some other way. After that happened, every time he came over, I had to go outside and play.

The first year on the farm, I couldn't go to the first grade of school because I wasn't old enough. The one-room school never had preschool or kindergarten at Hickory Grove. I remember one time that I asked Mom if she ever read the Bible; at times, she taught Sunday school.

Living on a farm, you learn about the birds and bees early; also I had a demonstration in Laramie.

Lloyd was a deacon in a Baptist church not far from the farm. The three of us were sitting on the first row of seats, Sis, Lloyd, and me. He told me to go outside and play with the frogs. The church building was built in the most tranquil place in the area, with full grown trees and a stream that flowed through the property. I will leave it up to you of what took place after I left the church, but I don't believe Sis was ever the same after that.

When we were left alone, Sis showed me how to do sex. I was five or six years old, and looking back, I blamed it on Lloyd; she must have been about eleven years old. In all the times I have heard about incest, it is usually between an older brother or father figure. Trust me, it happens between an older sister and a younger brother, with the girl as the instigator. At my age, I couldn't perform as well as if I was older, but I did the best I could with what I had. The reason that I bring it up is, in the families, parents don't know what is going on their children, and some of the incest is impossible to prevent. I told Paul what we were doing, but he gave me a blank stare as if it never registered, and I told him, "She would probably give some to you." As far as I know, he never got any sex from Sis. We did other things, such as who could urinate the furthest, which I always won; I had the advantage of being higher off the ground.

Dad had bought forty acres of land, about a mile from the farmhouse. World War II had ended, and he quit the railroad the second time. Years later, I found out that he was going to grow strawberries. The acreage consisted of trees, and more trees. With only one good horse out of the three, a hand saw, and double-bitted ax, he started cutting down trees at the first corner. It was Sis's and my job to cut off the branches, then to burn them up. Lloyd saw the smoke and knew Sis was working. He came over, and it wasn't long until I noticed I was working by myself. I went to find Sis and found Lloyd lying on top of her. I went back to the work area. Not long ago, I asked her about it, but she said she couldn't remember.

One time, Leroy (Dad's brother) was visiting, and Dad left the forty acres without me at quitting time; I had gotten lost in the woods. Dad went to the house without me and asked him, "Where is Mickey?"

"The hogs must have eaten him," he said. Mom picked up the pot of stew and threw it. Our supper went all over the floor.

Leroy said, "I think I'll go home now."

Walking in s straight line, I knew I would eventually get out of the woods. As I came out of the trees, they drove up. When we arrived home, they scraped the supper off the floor, and we ate after Dad thanked the Lord.

A man who came home from the war that lived not far away killed his wife, three kids, and himself. I'm not sure if Lloyd had anything to do with that or not. I never did hear why Lloyd wasn't in the army.

Lloyd was a great help to Dad and Paul on how to farm with horses. He showed Dad the way to castrate hogs, steers, etc.; that made them grow bigger and fatter. He also played the piano very well. There were two things the family was good at: going to church and, because they never believed in doing much else, teasing the children. Paul told me if you put salt on a bird's tail, they can't fly, and instead of wiping your butt in the outhouse with a sheet out of the Sear Catalog, use a corn cob. Neither one worked very well, for I tried both. It always went better if the catalog was wet after it rained; I found that out on my own. Paul told me he was circumcised at the age of eleven, and that made me either four or five. I know what they were talking about. They never did have me circumcised, and the reason Paul had it done was because it's mentioned in the Bible. The Jews were circumcised, and it is common practice today but not necessary, but you have to work at keeping the area clean.

Next door, there were a family of Cherokee Indians with a chubby daughter. To my knowledge, they never did any farming but lived well off oil well money from the government. One day, I started walking home from the first grade school, and they stopped the car and I got in and they took me home. The family was out on the front porch when I got out of the new car, and they kidded me so much that I walked hoe through the fields after that.

To get the hair off a hog, with my limited knowledge, I believed you only need hot water splashed on the skin and a knife to scrape the hair off. Dad killed a hog with the .22 riffle and gutted it. Then he laid it in a perfect spot next to a fifty-five-gallon barrel of water with a fire under it. He put a wheel in the tree, with a rope through it, and attached it to the hog. When the water boiled, he went to the barn and got a horse. The horses were as scared of Dad as they were afraid of the fire. When he came in the barn, they would shake. After attaching the rope to the horse, he said, "Getty up." The horse jolted forward, and the hog went up to the wheel. The rope broke, sending the hog down into the boiling water. The horse went back to the barn, and I went someplace else to play. As I was leaving, he pushed the barrel over to separate the water from the hog. Hearing a preacher cuss wasn't what I wanted to hear. Dad attempted the same thing, with the same result at the second farm. Albert Einstein defined insanity as "doing the same thing over, and expecting different result."

On Saturday, we usually went to Seneca to spend what little money we had. Dad gave Paul a dollar, Sis fifty cents, and me a quarter. Mom would try and buy a flour sack with the same pattern as she got the week before to make a dress for herself or Sis.

On the way to town, Dad would shut off the motor and coast down the hills, as a way to save gas, and for years, I thought everybody did that. At the bottom of the hill, he would put the car in a gear and let the clutch out to restart the engine.

Mom and I went shopping at the big store, and when we came out, Dad was walking towards us. I said, "New shoes, Daddy, new shoes." They were bought at the Salvation Army. After I spent my quarter, I would tell the family if they gave me a penny or nickel, I could buy a bigger candy bar, and that usually worked.

In Seneca was the first black person that I had ever seen, in a grocery store, either dressed like Aunt Jemima or she was aunt Jemima, giving out samples of cake or pancakes. Dad noticed the surprise on my face and walked me down about a block to a bridge over creek. On a tree next to the creek, a rope was tied to a limb. He said the last black person that stayed overnight was hung with that rope. Aunt Jemima had to be out of town by sundown.

Sis had begun piano lesson in Laramie, Wyoming, and her first teacher hit her across the hand with a ruler. Mom found out that the neighbor next door gave piano lessons, so she took them from her until we left. In Seneca, she found a teacher and would hitchhike from the farm for her lessons. When we moved to the second farm in Miami,

Oklahoma, she never took another lesson but did became a good piano player.

When we move from Laramie, Wyoming, to Seneca, it wasn't long after Dad had beaten me. In the area were a lot of Dad's relatives, and we had Sunday dinners together. The first time we were together, one of the women had newborn baby. A lot of attention was being given to the baby, so I went outside, got a stick, came back in the house, and poked the baby's eye out. Having already, had a beating to last a lifetime. No one did anything to me. The relatives never knew about the beating, and it was probably that experience that caused me to do that.

When I was six years old, I was allowed to go into the first grade. The grade school was Hickory Grove, with about seven grades, two miles from the farm. Sis and I both went there in 1943. The teachers during that period had to be single to teach school, and very few women drove a car.

During the year, the teacher told a boy to go outside and get some willow switches. The teacher made the kid stand up in front of the classes, and she beat him. I thought, *that was the same thing that happened to me, it must be normal.* A year ago, I asked Sis of she remembered what the boy did. She told me that he put a rifle bullet in the coal bucket that was used for the potbellied stove. I never did anything to rile the teacher through thirteen years of school after that happened. One of the other kids saw him put the bullet in the coal bucket and told the teacher.

Before Dad went to work on the railroad in Kansas City, I'm not sure if he found a church to preach in or not. The way it works, you preach in a church, and if the congregation or boards of directors like you, they will accept you as their pastor.

I believe it was the first church that the preacher preached in that Dad said Paul acted up; he left the pulpit, grabbed Paul by the arm, took him outside, and gave him a spanking. He came back in, went back up to the pulpit, and finished his sermon. They never asked him to come back, but it certainly worked with me after he beat the homosexual tendencies out of me. God called him to preach.

After the church service was over, I was standing by Paul on the outside. When Dad came out, Paul said, "Dad, I will never go to church again." I thought that was a death sentence, but he never said anything. He missed out on a lot of the dinners that we had with the relatives. I'm not sure what dad told them was the reason that Paul never went to church. I asked Sis recently if she knew why Paul never went to church with us, and she said she never knew.

One of the churches where he was accepted, he was moving a piano to the church with a truck. He never tied it down, and it tipped over out onto the road. He said because it was so heavy, he didn't think it would tip over. Another time, in a church service, he got carried away and told Sis and me to come up on the platform to help him sing the song. The only problem he had was neither one of us knew the words. The other problem he had was one time, mom told him that she couldn't get my neck clean for the Wednesday night service. He lay me down on the floor and planted his knee on my chest, and he not only cleaned my neck but damaged my vocal cords.

There was a windmill at the back of the house with no brakes, and it provided DC current to a couple of lights Dad had built a kitchen on the back of the house. A thunderstorm came up, and he had me down on the floor with my head in his crotch, flinging me side to side, and he called it playing and having fun. Sis was outside banging on the back door because the rain had swelled the door where it wouldn't open. As we "played" on the floor, she started running towards the front door, and the blades of the windmill fell behind her.

There was a huge beautiful tree in the front yard, and Mom saw a ball of lightning coming down the top of a barbed-wire fence. When it got to the corner, the ball of lightning jumped over to the tree and killed it.

The previous owner of the farm left a radio that worked on a twelve-volt system. You had to unhook the battery from the car and hook it up to the radio in the house. Because Dad was the preacher, the only thing that was legal to listen to was the heavyweight boxing championship matches. Joe Louis at that time won all of them, but Dad wasn't home all the time. Paul would bring in the battery, and we would listen to Fibber McGee and Molly, Lone Ranger, gone Hornet, Little Red Riding Hood, the Squeaking Door, and the Grand Old Opera, and so on.

On the farm, we always had Model A Fords with the rumble seat behind the cab, and that was where the kids rode most of the time. When we were going someplace, I tried to get in the rumble seat by myself. If I never made it there in time, Dad would lift me by one arm and put me in the seat; that felt good. He did that up to when I was at least eight years old. He liked to throw mw up in the air and

19

catch me on the way down. That was more fun; that makes your ribs feels good after you get older.

The offering on the churches never was more than seven dollars, and it was his weekly salary. We depended a lot on Ma's egg money. She made more money than Dad did in the church. Each spring, she would buy baby chicks that were used for either fried chicken or laying hens. With no refrigeration, most of the time they had to kill them as needed for supper. They cut the heads off with an axe and let them flop around on the ground. When I was there, Dad would show me how it was done the man's way. He would grasp the chicken by the head and twist if off by twirling it around. If that never worked very well, he would put his shoe on its head and pull the heads off. That was really impressive.

Wednesday night, we went to church, and he backed out of the garage without a door. When we arrived at the church and got out, a chicken was frozen, sticking to the top of the car, the meal for the next day, and who says the Lord doesn't provide after a little prayer? A Model A had stopped running out on the road in front of the house. I went out there and the guy was holding on the spark plug wire after he got it started, to see if there was any juice coming through. He was trying to find out which spark plug or wire was bad. He showed me how to do it, and that really impressed me. It was only twelve volts, so I never died.

The first ranch was next to worthless, so they started looking for another one for Paul to Farm. One of the farms that they looked at that they couldn't afford, they saw a Model A Ford in the weeds, and the farmer probably gave it to them. Paul took the motor out of the Ford that Dad had wrecked and put it in that one. It even had an electric starter, so now he never had to crank it to get it started.

Paul got another Model A from someplace, and he took the body off, the front seat out and the floor out. After he took it for a test run, he drove up and asked me, "Do you want to go for a ride, Mickey?"

After getting in it, I put my bare foot down on the hot exhaust pipe. About the only time I ever wore shoes was to church and school. Seldom if ever am I without shoes unto this day.

On Saturday when we went to town, Dad sold can of milk, half-and-half, to the dairy. He filled the can up with water because we were a little short of milk.

Mom canned from the garden enough to last a year. We always had dill pickles after supper. I would put a pickle in a slice of bread with mustard for a snack. Another thing I ate was a slice of bread with butter, sugar, and honey or molasses on it. One of the things that was only reserved for me was boiled chicken feet. Neither of the other siblings said they ever ate them. When Mom made a pie, she out the trimmings in the oven with nutmeg, and that was a good snack.

In winter, Paul cut blocks of ice from the river or pond, stored it in the cellar and covered it with straw. If they had any money, they bought blocks of ice on Saturdays for the ice box, but most of the time, we never had any ice.

Chickens, ducks, and domestic rabbits, we had to kill them as needed. When Dad acquired a hind leg of a pig, he rubbed either salt or sugar on the outside skin several times to preserve it. He attached it to a rope in the barn, and more than once, the starving barn cats would knock them down. He would wash the ham off, and what was left, we would eat. When he got rich, after church on Sunday night, we would stop at a café and order a bowl of chili and a Pepsi Cola. Sis remembered that also.

Lloyd gave me a rat terrier dog, but Dad gave it back when we moved to the farm near Miami, Oklahoma. Neither dog ever got a meal in their life. Paul found a huge turtle that might have been one hundred and fifty years old. Lloyd ran over it with a horse and wagon until it was mush. I'm not sure how it stayed away from the wrath of man for so long.

Paul was cleaning his .22 rifle in the kitchen, and Mom was sitting in a chair against the wall. Mom said, "I think I'll start supper," and when she got up, the gun went off, and the bullet went through the chair, about the height of her heart.

Chapter 4

FARM IN MIAMI, OKLAHOMA

We stayed one night with Lloyd and his wife, Bulea May, at their farmhouse. The next morning, we left to go to Miami, Oklahoma. Because of the man that came home from the war and killed his family, I was hoping that Dad never found out about Mom and Lloyd. People don't give enough credit for ids figuring things out what is going on, and I had a good demonstration on Laramie.

We moved in the middle of the third grade and at the end of the year, the teacher said I was too dumb to go to the fourth grade. My niece was in the same grade, and now she was a grade ahead of me, so the relatives had one more thing to ridicule me about.

Everything was the same in the conditions of necessary living at the new farm, except Paul had more dirt to grow more weeds. Sometimes, the cow's milk would taste like weeds. That wasn't conductive to Dad's milk route in Miami.

The first thing that I did was go up in the second level of the barn, if you could call it that, and my foot slipped off a two-by-four, and it met my crotch. I never said anything about that until now.

From the second level, there was an opening to the outside that dropped about fifteen feet. Paul took a barn cat to show me that if you drop a cat upside down, it will turn over in the air and land on its feet.

By this time, Paul must have been fourteen years old. He plowed the field the old-fashioned way, with a two-horse-drawn, single-blade plow. Dick was the only good horse; Duke would give Dick all the work, if he thought he could get away with it. Prince pulled the wagons, and Paul rode him a few times. Prince reached over the fence and bit my arm and Sis's shoulder. I have a lump in my muscle tissue in my arm to this day.

After plowing the field, Dad had a long board, about sixteen feet long, with spikes protruding out of the bottom, and it leveled the dirt. He stood in the middle of the board to control the horse, where the chain was attached. I came along and asked him if could have a ride. He said, "Hop on," and my weight pushed the spikes down into the dirt. The plank stopped and then it went forward, leaving me sitting in the dirt. I'm glad I never fell forward. Dad thought it was hilarious.

Mom, with only good leg, did more than her share of the work. She planted the garden after it was plowed and leveled it off. She did the canning, meals, and laundry, most of the time by hand on a washboard. She kept the house clean, started the fire in the potbellied stove in the morning and ironing with heavy irons heated on the cookstove. Dad had to look good, when he preached on Sunday. Sis or I turned a crank to make the cream separator work. Nowadays, people drink what is left, the 2 percent or no fat milk, but we fed it to the hogs. Somehow, butter was made. Most of the bread was homemade: pies, cakes, candy, and cookies. She made snow ice cream, and I don't think that was very healthy because a flake of snow forms around a particle of dust or salt. If I remember right, you put vanilla extract in it.

Dad bought a hay bailer that required a horse (Prince) to walk in a circle attached to a long pole; that's what made the bailer work. It was my job to keep Prince moving around the circle, with no shoes. I had to save my shoes for church. It damaged the nerves at the bottom of my feet. The hay wasn't bad to walk on; it was the weed stubble that tore my feet up. When Dad saw that all the stubble was flattened down, he moved the bailer to another location, and the pain would begin again. The weeds, with a little hay, after it was cut, was raked over to the bailer. With a pitchfork, the hay was put in a hopper by Dad or Paul. There was a reciprocating plunger that pushed the hay out into a square tube. The hay had to be tied with twine into manageable bails; that was done with Sis on one side and Mom on the other.

One time, Paul was pushing the hay down the hopper with his foot, and it went in too far because of the plunger reciprocating. He was lucky that Prince was the energy source. I only had to tell her to stop once; she was so lazy.

Another time, Paul was cutting the hay, and he thought he cut a finger off. He wrapped it in a rag, and blood was all over the outside. He told Dad that he cut his finger off. They left for Miami, and when they arrived at the doctor's office, he took the rag off and put a Band-Aid in the cut.

One of the neighbors wanted their hay bailed, and Dad decided to put the hay on the wagon instead of moving the bailer. I was sitting on the top of the hay when Mom came walking up. She told Dad to get me off the hay, which I did. When the wagon went from the field to the road, there was a slight incline, and the wagon tipped over, with the hay landing in a barbed-wire fence. The horses were spooked and left the area, pulling the wagon on the side; as we called it, a runaway pulling the wagon to obliteration.

Only one man ever rode Dick, and Paul bet Dad that he could ride him for five dollars. Paul plowed a field and never gave Dick any feed nor water all day. Mom happened to look out the window when she saw Dick fall down with Paul killed the horse. He got him up and rode Dick to the barn; he got his five dollars.

Sis was told to go and cut the head off a chicken for supper. She only cut half of its head off with the axe, and it ran under a shed and was hard to retrieve.

She was splitting wood, and the double-bitted blade of the axe never went all the way through the block of wood. Trying to help, I put my right foot down on top of the blade that was sticking up; it almost cut three toes off. Mom put kerosene on my foot until the next Saturday when she got some peroxide.

On the fourth of July, they would fry a chicken for picnic. They would buy pop, watermelon, and a buffalo (cantaloupe) for me. On one of the picnics, I must have said I wanted a buffalo, and from then on, it stuck. Every year, I would miss one day of school; I would be nauseated with a bilious problem in my stomach; with some of the food we were eating, I can understand why. It never lasted longer than about the time school was out; Paul and Sis thought I was faking, but Mom knew better.

Paul was riding Prince from the field to the barn, and Dad had put a fence across the path. Prince saw the fence went sideways, and Paul went off on his head, knocking himself out. Mom thought he was dead, but in a little while, he seemed okay, but Paul doesn't remember falling off the horse.

Mom would fix a lunch that we took to school, and one day, I hit one of my classmates on the head with my hard-boiled egg to break the shell. It wasn't a hard-boiled egg, and the substance slowly went down his face. At the time, if kids said they were sick, they got a spoonful of castor oil, but Mom had an onion syrup that I took that usually cured me.

Paul was driving the horse loaded with hay, and I was sitting on top. The horses got spooked and started to run away, and Paul said to dive off. I gave it my best dive, right into the ground, head first. If it wasn't for the straw hat that I had on. I might have gotten hurt. To this day, I can't dive into water or tumble over rolled-up mats. In high school, the bell rang when it was my time to tumble, and we were dismissed.

One time in the outhouse, there was about a six-inch worm hanging out my rectum. Sis was close by, and I yelled for her to go get Mom and Dad! They took me to a doctor in Miami, and he pulled the worm out the rest of the way. Dad was talking when he was about eighty years old and being taped with VCR.

He said that we were eating the same bran that he was feeding the horses. Then it all made sense.

Travelling to church, I told Dad that I was getting carsick, sitting in the middle of the front seat of a Model A Ford. He wouldn't stop, so finally I lunged across the seat toward the open window across my mother's lap. When Dad noticed me, he put on the brake and turned the steering wheel to give me more momentum to the window. My body hit the dashboard, and my head went into the top of the door. I still have the knot on my forehead to this day.

We were so poor that on Christmas, Aunt June (Mom's half-sister) would bring a box of stuff for Paul and Sis. She never could get it in her head that my parents had a third child; either that, or I looked too much like Dad, as she hated him with a passion. Aunt June was told to leave one of the southern cities because she was charging for sex instead of giving it away during World War II. Dad might have asked her for a freebie; he told me she was the prettiest woman that he had ever seen.

When we drew names at school at Christmas time, I always gave a box of chocolate-coated cherries, and I received a white handkerchief. At the Christmas plays, the kids would get the teacher so frustrated that she would break down and cry. When we first started about the third grade, the teacher told us, "I have heard you make the teacher cry practicing the Christmas play, but you're not going to make me cry." She was the worst one that cried that we ever had; even I felt sorry for her.

When they bought the second farm, Paul found a bow and arrow in the house. He took it outside and shot the arrow straight up into the air. When it came down, it would stick in the ground. I'm still here, so it never stuck in my head.

After the preacher would remodel the churches that he was accepted at, he would be asked to leave. He couldn't remember going to school. We would try and get invited after the Sunday service for dinner because of the distance back to the farm. One of the families has as many cats on the kitchen table as they had kids. They tried to avoid them. One Sunday, there was a new family in the congregation, and they invited us to their farm. It wasn't long after we got there that the man started putting his hand down my pants to squeeze my penis. He did it so many often. When dinner was ready, Mom made me up a plate and I ate out in the barn. After dinner their son took me out in the barn, and shoved his arm in the vagina of a mare. He let me do it, and when we got home, I told Paul what we did. He told me, "You should have washed your arm off first." As we drove away from the farm, the preacher said to Mom, "Maybe we should have said something to him or left."

Paul graduated from Wyndot High School, with Dad's suit coat and Leroy's pants.

Paul had rabbits, guinea hens, calves, and had bought a jersey bull to raise more milk cows. The bull got after me one time, but I beat it to the fence. A jersey bull is mean. A range bull in Wyoming, the only time I made one mad, was when I pulled it out during a fishing trip and urinated in front of his cows. I had never seen anything like it before. He ran at me and even clawed the dirt with his front feet.

I'm not sure how or why a fight took place, but Dad had Paul on the floor, Sis got on top of Paul and told Dad to hit her instead of Paul. When the fight was over, Dad told Paul that there wasn't enough room on the farm for two men.

Before Paul left, he said some of the animals were his, and Dad told him they are not. He said, "They have been eating my grass." Paul never did receive any financial compensation for anything for all his hard work. Paul went to Bettendorf, Iowa, to a farm; his aunt June was living in Davenport. He got mixed up with the farmer's daughter, and the farmer ran him off; afterward, he got a job with a construction company.

He bought a 1947 Cushman Motor Scooter, so when that job didn't last long, he asked Dad to come and get the scooter. Paul joined the United States Air Force, and I'm not sure why he never resold the scooter. Dad went to get it, and he put it in the rumble seat of the Model A Ford and took it back to the farm.

Paul was the farmer, Dad was the preacher, and Mom knew that she had a problem when the farmer was run off.

She asked the preacher if he would consider becoming a carpenter. He had remodeled almost all the churches that he was accepted at. He had built a taxicab office in Miami, remodeled the farmhouse in Seneca, and built the new house in Laramie. She told him that we could go to church wherever we lived.

During this period, the churches never had a doubt that the world was going to end with Jesus coming back the second time. There was the Dust Bowl of the '30s and World War II, but it never came to an end. I believe dad wanted to be behind a pulpit when the end of the world came.

When Dad told her he would do it, you probably could have knocked my mother ever with a feather. Mom didn't realize the hell on this earth that she would have to endure, as he always blamed her for getting him away from preaching.

They decided to sell the farm and went to Tulsa, Oklahoma, to buy a Spartan trailer after they gave most of their personal stuff away. A utility trailer was loaded up on the farm with our worldly goods in it, and on the way to Tulsa, they took it with them. They left it with them because I had pink eye. On the return trip back to the farm with the new Spartan trailer, he went by the auctioneer to get his money. He told them it rained all day and nothing was sold. He left all the stuff there and gave it to him, then he drove on to the farm.

While we were in school, Dad took Rex out on the pasture and shot him; his misery finally came to an end. At least twice, Rex came shot up from a shotgun blast. Yet he managed to survive. He was probably looking for something to eat. If Rex got a proper burial, it would surprise me. Most of the time, we never had any flea powder, and I could see fleas crawling all over the dog, literally eating him alive.

They parked the trailer just up the road from the schoolhouse, and it might have been the only time Dad waited for the school year to end. The day after my third grade ended, for the second time, we left, putting the fuel oil barrel and scooter in the front room of the trailer. I'm not sure where it came from, but Sis and I had a back seat to sit on out of the rain. Mom told the teacher that when we got toe wherever we were going, she would write a letter and have the grades sent to our new location.

Chapter 5

BOOMER

A boomer in construction is a person that goes from job to job, and the bigger the job, the better, that really needs men. They are not too picky about what is in your head or the experience that you have had. We went to Davenport, Iowa, where Dad got a job with John Deer Farm Machinery Company. Aunt June was living in Davenport, not far from Bettendorf. We parked in a trailer park where the tenants had beer parties on weekends and during the week if they felt a party coming on. They never did understand why my parents never drank.

One of the little girls my age was named Karen. I told her if she would show me hers, that I would show her mine. She showed me hers, and I went home. We lived not too far from the Mississippi River, and I cut a limb off a tree, the longest one I could find, to make a fishing pole. With a lunch and some catfish bait that Mom made out of flour and water. I discovered the fish weren't biting that day.

There was some kind of program where the kids made things out of plastic strips braided together for the kids who lived in the trailer court. When I got the hang of it, the car was backed up to the trailer hitch.

Dad couldn't stand prosperity. He either quit or was fired, and Mom had to send another letter back to the school to hold up on sending the grades. The carpenter business agent in Davenport told Dad that in Pekin, Illinois, there was a carpenter job (I believe it was on dam job) that needed men. When we got there, he showed the business agent the house in Laramie, Wyoming, that he had built. He said he would give Dad a journeyman carpenter card, if he was too old to go into an apprentice program. He had to learn the carpenter trade by trial and error, which is the hardest way to learn. The first thing he complained about was the boss told him to turn his nuts over; a nut has a flat side and a round side. He would usually catch the first layoff, and at that time, either there was no unemployment insurance money or he never applied for it. When he was fired or laid off, he would go to the business agent and ask them where another big job company trailer court, and you couldn't see a tree when you looked in any direction. It was part of his plan to make Mom stew as much as he could. She couldn't drive a car, so she had to endure the hot trailer house all day. The Spartan trailer never had any insulation in the walls, and the bedding would freeze to the walls in the winter.

In the grade school in Pekin, my grades from Hickory Grove hadn't caught up with us yet, and they had two different segments of pupils. One look at me, and they put me in the lower ranking group. When my grades did come, they decided they had made the right choice. I must have been as dumb as I looked.

It wasn't long after we got there that Aunt June (Mom's half-sister) and Ray, who was a carpenter, moved there. They rented a house not too far from the grade school. Sis would drive the scooter to June's house, then we walked to school, as
we never wanted the kids bothering the scooter. In my thirteen years of going to school, I never rode a school bus.

In the classroom, every time I had to speak, every kid in the class turned around and looked at me, as I usually set

34

on the back seat. At first, I couldn't understand what they were looking at, but eventually, I figured out it was my Southern accent, so I got to where I dreaded to speak. The teacher would have to call on me to get me to say something; I certainly never volunteered any information that she needed to know. The teacher was on her own.

Our assignment for homework was to draw a map of United States. I put a map next to me on the kitchen table, drew the map and when I gave it to the teacher the next day, she said I was lying. She said I traced it. I asked mom what the word trace meant, as I never went to preschool or kindergarten.

Mom never had to suffer very long because we came home from school, and the car was hitched up to the trailer. If we made any friends, we never saw them again. To this day, it has been hard for me to make friends.

From Pekin we went to Morton, Illinois, where I reentered the fourth grade, and we waited for my grades once more. Sis contracted rheumatic fever and missed so much school that she had to take the tenth grade over again. From Morton, we went to Galena, Illinois, and going into the town, there was a hill that we were going down. I'm not sure how many of us came out of it alive. Behind the steering column, there were two wires to apply the brakes on the trailer. The car never had any brakes, the way Dad was yelling. He must have gotten the trailer brakes on with the two wires that saved us from the crash. The only thing I know for sure was he wasn't asleep.

The closest thing we had for a bathroom in the trailer was a commode that you had to push down on a lever with your foot to release the waste, directly in the sewer. To my knowledge, there was no sewage trap, and the sewer gas came up into the trailer. The only other thing that was in the bathroom was a small sink. It was nice when we parked in a trailer court. I would have a place to take a shower, and it would be hooked up to a sewer pipe. What I really needed was a toothbrush.

In Galena, they couldn't find a trailer court, and somehow, they found a gasoline service station that let us park the trailer not far from a bathroom located at the back of the filling station. It never had a sewer hookup, so Dad put a bucket under the sewage pipe. The lavatory sink was bigger than the one on the trailer, so we used their sink and commode to take a bath most of the time, unless there was an emergency. He connected a water hose from the gas station to the trailer. For heat, the furnace used fuel oil that was in a fifty-five-gallon barrel. The cookstove used two propane bottles attached to the front of the trailer behind the hitch. Dad emptied the bucket into the commode inside the gas station rest room every day, or as needed. He had a pole installed for electricity.

On the other side of the gas station was a café that had a nickel slot machine, and it gave some of Sis's and my money to the management. At the time, I was riding the Cushman Motor Scooter, and with the gas in the tank plus the slot machine, it forced me to go to work. Not far from the service station was a golf course, and I caddied there when I wasn't going to school. I must have been nine years old, and with no knowledge of the game, when they handed me the score card, I had to tell them I never knew how to keep score. All I did was carry the bag.

One time, one of the golfers asked me, "How much money do you charge for eighteen holes?"

"Sometimes, they give me a dollar," I replied.

I made more money selling golf balls that I would find from previous players. Women practicing hitting the balls was the easiest money; all I had to do was put the balls in a bucket and carry it back to them.

Dad got a job working in the underground lead and zinc mines, and he told them that he had carpenter experience, but they gave the carpenter work to his future son-in-law, Merlyn.

At the mine, Dad must have had a place where they took a bath. Every Saturday evening, they gave me a washcloth to go take a bath in the sink at the gas station.

We moved two or three times when I was in the fourth grade to different towns in the Midwest, I learned to keep any possible friends at arm's length.

In the underground mine, a large rock fell and hit Dad on the head. It busted his hard hat. The new hat the company gave him was out in a shed and still have it.

It wasn't long after that happened, we left Galena, but I finished the fourth grade. In all the schools and churches, my greatest fear was the Christmas plays because at that time, it scared me to death to think I could end up with a speaking part. In all the plays that I dodged, they always made me into an angel, for they never had to say anything.

The business agent in Galena gave Dad two towns to go to for carpenter work. The first one was Sioux City, Iowa, and the other was Pierre, South Dakota.

We got to Sioux City and a few men in a car were harassing us. They were driving ahead of us or driving real slow on the hills, and at times, they were driving behind us.

Dad had already lost most of his teeth when he was about twenty-one years old, then he stopped the car, and asked a man what the problem was? The man hit him in the mouth with brass knuckles, and he told the dentist to pull the rest of his teeth out. He had a full set of upper and lower plates so that might have had something to do with why he never saw any need to buy us children a toothbrush. Half of my teeth were black, so I never showed much teeth uncles the occasion called for it.

We never stopped In Sioux City, Iowa, but went on to the second town on the list, Pierre, South Dakota. Later in my life I was driving through Sioux City and I was looking for a sign that said Gas at the next turnoff. I never did see a sign, so I drove through Sioux City the second time without stopping. I found out later that it was against the law to advertise for anything on the interstate in Iowa.

When we arrived in Pierre, we parked the trailer in a trailer court with a washhouse; it had commodes, sinks, mirrors, and showers.

Dad went to work as a carpenter, and Mom got a job in a commercial laundry. It was the first time she worked since we left the farm. Nothing during that time ever lasted every long. The manager of the trailer court noticed that I was riding the scooter around and around the trailer court. The manager said that he thought he would miss us when we left.

We moved the trailer to another trailer court; it was closer to school anyway. I never needed any license to drive the scooter, but I stayed out of the trailer court and rode it on the street and highways. My biggest trip that I took was going from Pierre to Fort Pierre. Every time I went over there, the saddle horse champion of the rodeo lived there, and I thought of him. I believe his name was Casey Tibbs.

In the trailer, Sis and I slept on a couch that had a back that dropped down; it was sort of rainbow in shape, and that was the part that she gave me to sleep on. It was hard as a rock and about that comfortable. For a change, when Dad was fired, he never hooked up the trailer and left town. Mom was working. It was the first time that I saw Dad fish. You could catch as many bullheads as you wanted. We ate them every day for supper. To this day, I can hardly stand to eat a bullhead.

Sis was in the tenth grade, and Dad thought she was spending too much time with the boys. It never helped when she told Dad to find a job when he was reading the Bible. She came to the house a little late, a time or two, from a date. Dad went to the police station and asked them to put her in the reform school. They told him the system never worked that way, that she had to commit a crime first.

She told me last summer that two men raped her in Pierre, and she told them that she wouldn't say anything, fearing for her life.

Sis packed what little she had in a suitcase and hitchhiked or rode a train back to Galena, Illinois, to Merlyn. When she arrived, she stayed at Merlyn's mother house, on their farm, until they were married, and she helped out with the chores.

For a little extra income after Sis left, Dad took me to a bowling alley to set the pins manually. The way that was done, a person had a place to stand while the bowling ball was rolled down the lane and knocked over the pins. Then you stepped down and set the pins back up. It wasn't unheard of that the pin setter at times would be hit by a pin. The only problem Dad had was the man at the bowling alley told him that they only bowled in the winter; it was still summer, and that made me happy.

In Pierre, I went to one Cub Scout meeting, but I never was much of a joiner. Most all the things that I played with was homemade. I made a slingshot out of rubber bands. Downtown in Pierre, at the Becker Drugstore was a huge sign with lights all over it. A bird was sitting on the top, the rock hit a little low, a glass from the sign came trickling down. The manager came out, and I could tell it hurt him beyond measure. I crossed the slingshot under my arms where he couldn't see it and walked away. There are some things in life that a person regrets, and this was one of them.

In the trailer court was a building that the management hired Dad to reroof. I laid the shingles down, and Dad nailed them, it was the first construction job that I worked on; I must have been about nine years old.

Sis sent us a notice in Pierre, South Dakota, that she was going to marry Merlyn, and the date, in Galena, Illinois, she became a Catholic because that was what Merlyn's family was. We drove back there, and after the wedding, the priest and Dad were drinking beer, which in most Protestant churches was against their doctrine. I knew it was against Dad's religion; I had to have learned something in the years of going to church. As we were driving back to Pierre, Dad said, "Well, the priest was drinking beer. If he can, I can."

When the Christmas play came, I was too late when they cast the parts. They made me into another angel, and I stood around until it was over with. We left Pierre when we came back from Sis's wedding, and I had finished the fifth grade, which was unusual in the same town. They traded in the old car that we left the farm in for a new 1948 Ford pickup. That is what you can buy when your women to go work. They had already traded in the Spartan trailer, and what was different about the new trailer was the bathroom had a shower with a drain hole in the center; the door was the shower curtain. Under the kitchen cabinets was a small electric hot water tank, but you had to use the water sparingly. Dad lived in this trailer for at least twenty years, following construction. It became known as the old green trailer. It was 29 by 8 feet wide, including the hitch.

When we left Pierre, we went to Sioux Falls, South Dakota, and parked it on an empty lot. He used a bucket underneath the sewer pipe like he did in Galena. With a building close by, he connected a garden hose from it and dumped the waste bucket as needed. One thing we did need was a pole for an electric meter, which he got hooked up.

Mom started taking courses to be stenographer, shorthand and typing, etc. it would be easier than working in laundry. When they said that she completed the course, she went and worked for a doctor. She couldn't remember anything that she was taught and he asked her if she would be the janitor; she did that until we left.

In Sioux Falls, South Dakota, I went to the sixth grade all year.

There was a stray dog that came by the trailer, and I asked Dad if I could keep it. The dog was a year or more old. And he said I could have it. He put the dog's tail on a block of wood and, with a butcher knife on the tail, hit the knife with a hammer. The next morning, the dog had left. What I needed to know is, which way had it gone?

We were parked not far from the Sioux River, and I had a lot of fun there. The railroad tracks were between the trailer and the river, where boxcars would be parked on the tracks. A lot of birds hung out around the boxcars that I killed with a BB gun. Bows were made out of a limb of a tree, and the arrows were weeds that I got along the river. A rabbit trap was made out of box with a door that fell down when they went inside. I turned them loose; it didn't seem right capturing them that way. A few times, I would catch a cat and have to make a new box.

When the river froze over, ice-skated, but my skates weren't the right kind; they were from the Salvation Army, according to Mom. They hurt my ankles.

There was a bar that was built near the river, and they had a loudspeaker in the outside of the building. Most of the time they played, "Goodnight, Irene."

Dad bought me a Winchester Pump 22, and I went hunting for a cottontail rabbits. It started running away from me, and I shot it on the run. The second bullet that came out of the gun hit it by accident. After I carried it home, probably at least two miles, I laid it down on the ground. Dad picked it up and put it in trash; it was a jackrabbit. The tension between my parents, I could cut it with a knife. Mom probably thought I was lying out in the country bleeding to death, and they had words to that effect. Dad had driven the truck out into the country and let me out; that was the problem.

When the inevitable happened and Dad lost his job, we went to Rapid City, South Dakota. On the way there, we stopped at the Corn Palace in Mitchell and Wall Drugstore; they were near the road. We seldom went out of our way to see anything; it seemed like money was always an issue.

We parked the trailer in a trailer court on Omaha Street. It had all the amenities of normalcy, but that never lasted forever. Dad was hired on a construction job at the Rapid City Air Force Base.

Chapter 6

THE END OF THE ROAD

Mom saw an advertisement in the Rapid City newspaper for someone to rent and clean the rooms daily at a motel. Martin's Motel was located at the end of St. Joseph Street, next to the School of Mines College. They said that the only time anyone ever stopped there was when all the other motel rooms were full.

The motel was built backward, with the front facing the back alley. From the street, all you could see was a plain wall. Someone was sitting on their thumb during construction, and by the time it was noticed, to was too late to change, according to the contractor.

The first Sunday, we attended the Assembly of God Church. When I came out from my Sunday school class into the main sanctuary, Dad and Mom were standing there.

Dad said, "Go get in the truck. We're leaving."

That was different. I couldn't remember being told those words after Sunday school. He backed the truck up in the parking lot and hit a telephone pole. Evidently, he had a different meaning of one of the scriptures than the teacher. That's the reason you see so many different Baptist churches. It might have been over salvation; the preacher always said that you had to pray through. But Billy Graham came up with a new version; he said all you have to do is believe, come to the front to get my literature, and go back to your friends. That version is emulated today, and someone added, "Repent." The churches like that word.

One of the little girls that lived close by took me to her house to meet her mother. When I was introduced to her, I smiled, and half of my teeth were black. She was really impressed with what her daughter had brought home.

In front of the wall from the Main Street, Dad parked the trailer. That never helped to rent the motel rooms. I'm not sure if we were hooked up to a sewer or not, as it seemed like half the time we weren't. In the vicinity of the motel, I met three or four playmates, and one of them I still communicate with today. We graduated from Rapid City Central High School in 1956, and I'm one of the few that still have their graduation ring. All we could afford was the girls ring, so it was a little small.

We stayed there about one summer, and Mom saw another advertisement in the Rapid City newspaper that said a lot with an unfinished house was for sale. Dad bought it, and the seller said that he would give us the woods forms to finish making the concrete blocks if we gave them back to him after we were done with them. He also said that he would lay the rest of the blocks as part of the price of the lot. He had about two layers of blocks already laid for the walls.

With Dad working at the base, he said that maybe I could make the blocks after school. He said he would show me how when we get a pole in the ground for electricity. He bought a cement mixer, and soon as we had electricity, he showed me how to put in a mixture of three, two, and one. Three shovels of aggregate of gravel, two sand, and one

45

cement. I put that proportion in the mixer along with the water. We ran a water hose from the Johnson house next door. I was eleven years old and in the seventh grade.

At first, I put the forms together with four number 9 wires; the blocks were two blocks, and they called it a dead-air space between them. The face side was slanted, and that made it look like drop siding when they were laid. The first day, I would put the mix in the forms. The next day, I would take the forms apart, and clean, oil, and set them up for when I got out of school the next day. All the concrete blocks were heavy, but the corner blocks were the heaviest; they required a different form. When we had made enough blocks to finish the house, Mr. Coon laid them the rest of the way.

When Dad wasn't there, I was the block layer's hod carrier or the one that carried the blocks and the mixture of screened sand, cement, and water to him.

Dad had made another outhouse on the lot for the hired hands, the bricklayer, and me. The trailer was going to be brought to the lot eventually, but I believe he waited until we had sewer line in.

My next chore was the sewer ditch. The backhoe couldn't dig out the ditch any closer to the wall because it was up already.

With a dull pick and shovel, I had to dig the ditch under the wall, from the front of the house all the way through and out the back for the trailer house.

With the sewer and water line in, he pulled the trailer over to the lot from the motel to finish the house.

He made his own windows out of two windows and storm windows he bought that were made out of aluminum. He never put any insulation in the walls; he said the dead-air space would be sufficient. Today, we would pour loose fill insulation down the blocks before the roof is put on.

On the inside of the house, he put Sheetrock on backward. He said the stucco would stick better. Normally, the Sheetrock was finished off by what we called per-pa-taping, but you have to put the good side out. When he put stucco on the ceiling and walls, he got almost as much on the floor. We screened the sand first, to mix water and cement with it in a homemade trough, then I would bring the mix to him.

He had already made a mess out of the roof in Laramie, so he asked Ray Keith, June's live in, to come to Rapid City and help him with that. Ray had more experience in the construction trade, and my middle name came from him.

The walls were so heavily made out of concrete that they withstood the 1972 flood of Rapid Creek. It was one of the few houses left standing in the area.

Christmas was around the corner, and Dad said, "Mick, you have been working a lot lately. Let's go downtown, and I'll buy you a new bike."

The three of us got in the truck, and we went down to Main Street at a hardware store. I picked out a swain one-speed bike, and I said to Dad, "I'll ride it home." It was only about four blocks to the house.

"No," he said, "put it out behind the truck." When he told me that, I parked it behind the truck and got in the middle of the seat with Mom. He came out of the store, started the truck, and backed over the bike. He got out, picked the bike up, and threw it in the bed of the truck. We went home. If everything went well, I wouldn't have wanted to scar up my new bike by putting it in the bed of the pickup. Evidently, that was what he wanted.

Dad never knew it at the time, but he was in trouble. This was the first time since the farm that Mom never had wheels under her house.

Ray had flown to Alaska in an airplane, and he sent Dad a letter that if he would drive his car up the Alaska Highway, which wasn't finished yet, there was carpenter work up here, but he had to bring June with him. When he arrived in Alaska, there was no work. He stayed a few days and rode a bus back to Rapid City, South Dakota. He never flew in an airplane, nor did I ever know of him getting a motel when he went on a trip. If he got tired he would stop the truck and doze off a little while in the front seat.

With Dad in Alaska, the homestead had changed. Mom started working at the Duck Inn Café, washing dishes, and had went out partying with one of the waitresses that she worked with. She was receiving twenty-five dollars a week before taxes. She had a picture of the waitress, and every time Dad saw it, he would say, "That is the woman that broke up my marriage." There were a lot of things that he

48

did that would break up a marriage, and in this book are a few.

When Dad came back from Alaska, Mom told him she wanted a divorce. She also loved the Black Hills just outside of the city; she had a weakness for green, and the Hills had plenty of that. They told me that I had to decide whom I wanted to live with. I never did tell them, so they decided that I would live with Mom and Dad would be my guardian. Because Mom filed for divorce, she had to get an appraisal on the house and pay Dad half of the appraised value; it came to $15,000. I was twelve years old, and because Mom filed for the divorce, they said Dad never had to pay any alimony or child support. Every Christmas, he would send me a five-dollar check.

The day after the divorce, he showed up drunk with a woman, and he told Mom she ruined his life. To understand that statement, you would have to know what the Bible says; of course, the king James of 1611.

"For if a man know not how to rule his own house, how shall he take care of the church of God?" (Timothy 3:5)

I don't believe in the validity of that statement, but for now, that is beside the point. I believe Dad believed that verse, and the next twenty years, he was drunk most of the time.

One of his bosses asked me one time if Mike was my dad. I told him yes, and he said he had to lay him off one time because he had a bottle on his toolbox.

When Dad was leaving, Mom asked him, "Before you go back to Casper, would you build me a hutch in the wall for the china that Paul sent me during the Korean War?"

The wall had a terrible curve in it anyway because of a curved stud.

The next day, he showed up to work on the hutch. He liked to have someone help him when he was working. All day, he cried, and from that day forward, I decided that I would never let love of another human being be a factor in my life.

The only transportation we had was the Cushman scooter or taxicab, so Mom took a taxi to work. I could get groceries on the scooter.

It wasn't but about five blocks to school, and I started in the seventh grade either riding my bike or walking to school. The paperwork was hell on wheels when it had anything to do with my parents. Dad was my guardian, so do I put his name down, but what do I put his name down, but what do I put down for an address? Most of the time, I never knew where he was or do I put my mother's name down? I know her address, but she's not my guardian.

She met Roy Palmer, and he brought her home at times from work. Because her right leg was normal, she could have driven a car her entire life, as long as it had an automatic shift. I blame everybody that was associated with her that never recognized that she was capable of driving a car.

Roy would buy cigarettes by the carton, and I stole them out of his car one package of Camels at a time. Later in life, he told me that he knew what I was doing, but he thought of it as the price he had to pay for going with my mother.

As long as I could remember, at the yearly physical exam in the different school, they would send a note home that I needed my tonsils out, and I never did pass the hearing exam very well. God knows my teeth were a nightmare.

After the divorce, she found out Dad had a little insurance through the carpenter local, and she finally had my tonsils out. She also started sending me to a dentist to have all my cavities filled. He would only do one tooth at a time, and I would always schedule the appointment during my drafting class. My grade out with a B, and I believe the next grade was D, then, three FFF's passing with an E.

After the divorce, Dad would come to Rapid City to work a few times. One time, he was there during deer season. I asked him if he would drive me toward Mount Rushmore about twenty miles and let me out. I wanted to go deer hunting. I told him when I wanted to come after me. He said he would, probably because if he never saw me alive again, he wouldn't have to send me five dollars for Christmas. I bought a deer license, and Paul had brought back a Korean gun with armor-piercing shells from the Korean War. The shells were against the Law, but that didn't bother me.

He let me out with my sack lunch, and after walking a couple miles, I set down on a log to eat my sandwich. A deer came walking slowly through the trees, and with careful aim, I fired the gun. It ran off. I was watching the deer, and in about a half block, it fell over.

After figuring out where I eventually got it to the road, I hid it in a ditch and walked to a phone to call Mom. If a hunter has noticed, I never cut its throat to bleed it, nor did I dress it out in any way. When Mom and Roy came, it was in the same shape as it was when it was born, except dead. I was thirteen years old.

Roy and I picked it up and put it in the trunk if his 1949 Chevrolet two-door coupe, closing the trunk lid. He must have been as smart as I was about hunting. We took it to a deer processing plant, and shortly after we got home, they called us on the telephone to tell us the deer was spoiled.

I had a few friends on the other side of town, but I never remember any of them coming over to our new house. Mom never wanted me to bring any friends to the house; she thought they would get me into trouble. At the Rex movie theater downtown, there was a movie advertised as being R rated; it was about a baby being born. From the theater to the corner of the Alex Johnson Hotel, about a block long, men were lined up to see it. When the big picture came to be, they had a sheet over her legs, and that view can be seen almost daily now.

One day, the cook never showed up for work, and they asked Mom if she could cook. That was when the waitress would yell to the cook all sorts of phrases that only God and the cook knew what it meant. Mom went from washing the dishes to professional cook and got a ten-dollar raise before taxes of $35 a week. My first job outside of selling pop bottles, with no retirement plan, was given to me through June, who was taking care of an elderly m an. One of his relatives had a farm near the city, and they needed help. Going out to the farm, they told me to cut the weeds down with that sickle over there. About three o'clock, I was finished. I went to the boss and asked him what he wanted me to do next. He took me to a three-foot-high wire fencing that he wanted rolled up. It was getting bigger every minute. It got to the point where I couldn't roll it anymore, but it was quitting time. The next day, I decided I was not man enough to roll up the fence, so I never showed up for work.

There was one job of landscaping, just enough to teach me to avoid that in the future.

I believe I saw an advertisement in the Help Wanted section in the newspaper, a greenhouse or nursery needed help. They were changing the rotted-out wooded beds where they grew most of the flowers. I would be working with a Sioux Indian man, and it would pay seventy-five cents an hour. It never mattered to me what nationality he was. I couldn't figure out when, or ever, he bathed. We had to tear down the old beds, and after a carpenter built new ones, we put dirt and fertilizer in a machine that ground it up. The machine was small enough it fit in the new bed; we pulled it along as needed. The management's conscience bothered them, and in about a week, they told me they would give me the same pay as the man of one dollar per hour. I was fourteen, making five dollars more per week than Mom, before taxes.

We kept telling the boss that we were getting an electrical shock when we touched the machine, and nothing was done about it. The condition must have been just right; when I touched the machine, it wouldn't turn me loose until they shut the electricity off. The side of my little finger was burnt, and when I came to my senses, they wanted to take me to the hospital, but I told them I was all right and went back to work.

At the Christmas party, they put whiskey in the eggnog, and that was my first drink. I liked it. I was only fourteen years old, and it felt good.

When we got the flower beds done, they laid the man off, and because they saw me come to work on the motor scooter, they asked me if I could drive a car. I told them no, and I followed him out the door.

The Sooper Dooper Grocery store was on my route when I went rabbit hunting on my bicycle, about five miles, and walked another five miles. At times, I had sold them pop bottles, and I never took any water with me rabbit hunting, so I would buy a bottle of pop going home. The mistake I made was going over the grocery store and asking them for job.

The Sooper Dooper market owners were from Pierre, South Dakota. They had just bought the store, and they hired me. I asked him how much do they pay, and I was told $125 a month, and I moved in, at least it felt like it. One time, I figured out I was making thirty-five cents an hour. Mom was making $19 more than I made a month. The hours that I put in were so much greater; it turned out to be my second home, or was it the third? The reason they never had a store out of South Dakota was they never had to adhere to any federal labor laws.

My main job was sacking groceries in paper sacks, and at times, I would carry out as many as four or five at a time, if they bought that much. When I got to some of the cars, I would have to open the door myself. It wasn't like it is now with carts that the customers wheeled out to the car, unless help is needed or wanted.

At first, I rode the scooter to the grocery store, but one day, I was travelling down New York Street to my house, and at about Sixth Street, a car came around the corner, at the second house, they turned left in front of me. I laid the scooter on the side and got on top of it. The back end of the scooter went under their back bumper; it never touched their car. Most of the skin on my left hand was gone, and the scooter never ran right after that. I don't believe those in the car knew what had happened, and it was their fault. It was the only accident that I ever had riding it in four years. When Paul came back from the Korean War, it was a wreck. He gave it to one of the men he worked with out at the Rapid City Air Force Base.

Through poverty, hardship, and conditions that I could not change, I'm not sure when my childhood turned into manhood.

It seems like I have traveled down the road alone, with people only temporarily in my life. Living on the farm, following construction, many different schools, the navy, where everyone on the ship is temporary. I learned how to make decisions early; perhaps I am a man. I question what you say and do; it doesn't matter to me where your idea or belief comes from: you, the Pope, or pauper. It is not in my record to be a joiner or be a part of a trend. Even in the navy, I never said a word in saying my allegiance to them;

it was said in a group setting. In other words, all my jobs were temporary, and if you really think about it, everything in life is temporary.

Chapter 7

A BOY TO A MAN

I'm not sure what happened between Roy Palmer and Mom; one day, he was history. Her next boyfriend was Art Beckner. He never smoked, so there went my free packages of cigarettes. He was the main grease mechanic at the Ford garage.

Dad had come from Casper and had brought his trailer; he was back working at the Rapid City Air Force Base. He parked the trailer about four blocks from the house. He came over to visit, and when he was about to leave, I said, "Dad, can I drive your truck to your house?"

He said okay, so I got behind the steering wheel and started it up. He showed me how to put it in reverse, a stick shift, but first pushing the clutch in, and backed it up out in the street.

Pushing the clutch in first, I put it in low, and we were off. On the way, I put it in second gear, and about the time we got to his trailer, it was in high or third gear. That was my driver's training, if you could call it that. He was reluctant to teach me how to drive because he could see Mom and I needed a car.

Art was working for the Ford Motor Company and saw a 1940 Chevrolet traded in for another car. They wanted $150 for it, and I had the cash.

It was the first day that I had the car, and I was travelling down New York Street where we lived. Six blocks from the house, a train was going by. As I was waiting for it to pass, a woman parked behind me. Then she backed up and went down a road next to the railroad tracks to the right, the train was going left. The train went by, and I proceeded to drive down the road. The very next intersection, the women's car and mine collided. She ran through a stop sign. She decided it was my fault and I would have to fix her car. We agreed to leave quietly without the police being called. I went over to tell my dad my woe, and she said, "What else is new." From then on, the back fender of my new car was caved in.

Rose lived about a block from me. We had dated a few times, and I took her to a Sooper Dooper Christmas party. When I got my first car, I took her to school and back home a few times. I believe I was in the tenth grade, and she was in the ninth grade of high school.

One day, Rose, another girl, her boyfriend, and I went up into the Black hills where we parked; the girls stayed in the car. The mistake I made was leaving the keys in the car. They assumed that we had other things on our mind that were not nice, so they locked the car and wouldn't let us back inside. I never had the tendency to force any girl to do what she never wanted to do. They threatened to walk back to Rapid City, but that made me concerned for their safety. We finally convinced them to let us drive them back home.

One day, when I took her home from school I said, "Tomorrow, I won't be taking you to school. I feel like I'm married to you."

I could see that a person could end up with three kids and a thirty-year mortgage. I had some living to do, and I had made a pledge not let love dominate my life.

My fiftieth high school reunion, the only one I ever attended, one girl came up to me and told me she remembered me.

A date for the junior or senior prom was not in the cards.

After we finished the house in Rapid City, Paul came back from the Korean War, and he had married a Japanese girl in japan. He asked to be stationed at the Rapid City Air Force Base (Ellsworth). With Dad's trailer gone behind the house, he bought a trailer and packed it in the same place.

They started having children, one after the other, and his wife had five. At the back end of Paul's trailer, he held a gallon of clear liquid and brought it to my nose. Paul said "Here, Mick, smell this." It was pure ammonia, and it almost knocked me to my knees.

When I was fifteen years old. Paul and I would go downtown to bowl. After we bowled, we started going to the 3.2 beer bars. In South Dakota, you only had to be eighteen years old, and in some of them, all you needed was the price of the beer. The first night, a couple of Indian girls sat at our booth. I liked that. The girls in high school never knew I existed. It became almost a daily thing, school or no school, that I spent most of my extra time in the bars. After the divorce, I sort of quit school but keep attending. Most of the subjects I took were drivers training or general math etc.

The next night, I went to the bar by myself. The girl that I was with the first night took me down to a hotel on Saint Joseph Street. When I went home, I threw my old bicycle away.

That left all the girls in high school virgins, including Rose, as far as I was concerned, for the rest of my schooling.

After we went bowling, sometimes we would go out the NCO club at the air force base. Because the drinks were so cheap, we would each order three drinks at a time. One time, the Ink Spots band was playing out there, and it wasn't beneath us sometime, for either or both of us to take a girl from the bar out there. With no supervision, I would go from motels to high school, beginning in the tenth grade. I was at least one year older than my schoolmates because of failing the third grade. Before Mom went to work at five a.m., she would have Art drive around to the motels to see which one I stayed at by locating my car, to see if I was still alive.

One morning, Mom woke me up and asked me if I brought home one of my girlfriends, as there was one out in the yard, sleeping under a man's overcoat.

One girl, when I asked her where her house was located, told me to take her to the tuberculosis sanitarium. That never sounded good. In the eleventh grade, I took industrial relations; in the graduation yearbook, that was all they could say about me. It consisted of working from one p.m. to ten p.m. on some nights. I was already working at the grocery store a couple years, so about all it did for me was give me more money for beer. We had a class about working for one hour during the morning. It was a bad situation, but at the time, it worked for me. It never left

60

very much time for any serious studies. College was never mentioned. All Mom wanted was to see me graduate from high school. Dad said he never remembered going to school; he had to help take care of his brother and sisters, two girls with four boys.

At the Sooper Dooper Grocery Store, because I was only making $125 a month, when school started, a few hours were removed from my total hours. They really had a problem, reducing my monthly wage. When I started working in the afternoon, they were happy. I got in as many hours as I did in the summer.

When I first started working there, I worked in the produce department. They never told me the main produce man never like kids. Sometimes, he would throw fruit at me, and he told me to sack potatoes from a hundred-pound sack. It was a death sentence if I never got twelve sacks at ten pounds each supposedly. If I had just belonged to a union, I could have told them. It doesn't bother me, the nonexistent wages; it is the fruit that I am complaining about. When I go over to a business for parts for my lawn mower, they have the eleventh commandment behind the desk, "Thou shall not whine." In back of Mom's house, about a half block, a company stored their produce, and it was delivered to the different stored from their trucks. I heard a truck coming down the road when I left the house to go to school. It had snowed in the night, so I made a snowball and sent it toward the road. The driver had his window down, and it connected on the side of his head. I found a different route to walk to the school. When I got to my job at one p.m., the driver was showing my boss where someone had hit him on the side of his head with a snowball.

Driving my 1940 Ford to the grocery store on Highway 79 by the School of Mines College, I was speeding as usual and I noticed in my rearview mirror the police car that went past me was turning around. I put the pedal to the metal and went around the curve. I noticed that the grease rack was empty at the gasoline service station. I drove the car inside the station. The cop had his pedal down as he went by and never noticed the car.

The station was the cheapest gas in town, twenty-six cents. I had bought $1 worth of gas for years there. And they put it in for me. My other purchase that was a must was a package of Pall Mall cigarettes, or big reds as we called them. Beer was not far off the list; it might have been at the top. The next day while everybody was sitting around on a coffee break, I told the troops the way that I ditched the cop. My boss walked over to me afterward and said, "Do you know who that man is over there?"

I said no.

"That is the cop."

He started working part-time, and we became good friends. I believe that was a felony, and I have two felonies left. I'm not sure how three felonies would have played out if I got caught in regard to joining the US Navy a few years later.

The second felony was when a few of us went to Deadwood, and as I went speeding by cop, I knew the narrow streets would handicap his turnaround. I went to the next street, turned right, parked and shut the lights off. He drove past me like he was looking for someone.

The same night, as I was coming back into Rapid City at the old Packard garage, a café was across the street. As I was going down the hill, I noticed a cop car facing the café and the cop running from the door to his car. I went on around the corner, turned right down a side street, parked, and turned off the lights. He had just had his donuts, he was working his lights, and siren, but his adrenaline was clouding his brain, he must have wondered where I went; it was the third felony.

Across the Rapid City High School, there was an open lot where we parked. After arriving at the school a little early, I put the 1940 Ford in a low gear and spun a 360-degree circle. When the dust cleared of the windshield, I noticed a cop car driving up. He gave me a ticket for careless driving but made the mistake of scheduling my court case during school hours. The judge wasn't happy about that, when I told him I was still in school.

It was almost yearly that I would destroy a car one way or another. I let a shade tree mechanic overhaul the 1940 Ford. When he was done, I was driving to work, and the heater almost steamed me out of the car. He must have put water in the radiator and it had frozen the heater. Another time, my right front fender as lying against the front wheel. I took the fender off. And driving to work, it was raining. It really didn't make any difference if I looked out the windshield or stuck my head out the side window. I couldn't see either way but managed to get to work.

In driver's training, they brought in a machine that timed the reaction time with your foot, going from the gas pedal to the brake, when the light turned red. I was the slowest person in the class.

Some nights, I never got any sleep; she would keep me up all night. Most of the girls that loved me were at least thirty years old, and most of them told me they wanted to be independent. That was all right with me; I never made a rule in my life.

One night, at a family dance hall, I got along well with one of the girls my age, and the next night, I made a date with her. When she got in the car, she was leaning on the door handle on the passenger side. I asked her, "What do you want to do?"

She said, "I don't care."

So I turned the car around and drove her back home; she got out.

Paul knew that I had went out a few times with a girl that worked in the meat department. He asked me, "Do you care if I went out with her?"

I told him it was okay with me. She went out with him, and the next day, he came up to me in the grocery store. "Mick, she never had any panties on."

I told him none of my girls wore any panties. On the TV the other day, they said it was almost normal for the girls on this day and age to go commando.

At the other store, one of the meat department women was separated from her husband. She knew I was working, and it was about closing time. She called me up, asked me

if I would come over to her house, and bring some beer. I bought a six-pack of Malt 45; that always did for me. The beer influenced us to lie down on the front room couch. Her husband told my boss that when he looked through the front window, his wife was on
the couch with me. He said he went over to his house with a bouquet of flowers to give to her.

Above Rapid City, on what we called Dinosaur Hill, most guys parked, if the need arose. After the bars closed, I took a girl up there on Skyline Drive; between passing out and love making, it was daylight when I started driving the car down the hill. The car stalled on the road, and a man stopped at the driver's side window. He asked if I needed a jump. I told him yes. About that time, my girlfriend raised her head up from the front seat and looked at him. He drove off. I told her, the next time someone stopped, keep your head down, if you know what I mean. A few cops stopped. They would wander over to the car and I would have to explain the birds and mosquitoes to them. "She is the bird that flies from one hitching post to the other, and I'm the mosquito that sucks the fluids out using a straw."

Next door to the Ford garage was a café that mostly catered to Indians. When they ordered a hamburger, they only wanted it seared on both sides and put in a hamburger bun. If all else failed during the night, that was a good place to go as a last resort. One night, one of the girls went out to the car with me. I told her to get in the back seat and take off her clothes while I drive to a place to park the car. When I parked the car, she was completely undressed, even had her shoes off.

Wayne Forman, who I worked with at the grocery store on highway 79, and I decided to go to Edgemont, South Dakota, to visit his parents in blinding snowstorm, after we had a few too many drinks. We left Rapid City about ten p.m. in the 1949 Ford that I drove in the twelfth grade of high school. That might have been the reason I never had a date for the prom. Coming back from Hermosa from a family dance, Dad rolled it with his girlfriend and another couple in it. He had paid $600 and I gave him $150. From the front to the back trunk lid, it was all dents or out of shape in one way or the other. We jacked up the roof using a 4x4 and a jack.

As we were going down the highway, we kept running into huge snow drifts, and I went through them with my trusty Ford. I saw a big drift coming to meet us. I pushed the pedal to the metal and went into the snowdrift at top speed. When the car came to a halt and the snow blew off the windshield in front of the car, an eighteen-wheel truck was stuck. Wayne said, "I'll get out and push you backward," and he put his back against the truck, but the car wouldn't move. The temperature got to five below zero. And we went to sleep. The next morning, the sun was shining; we hitchhiked back to Rapid City and got one of our friends to bring us back out to get the Ford. The Snowplow had even taken the snow out from under the car. We drove it back to Rapid City; Wayne's parents would have to wait. The manifold exhaust pipe had come off the engine of the Ford, and the noise couldn't get any louder.

Showing the boys my proficiency on a pool table, I came out of the pool hall on St. Joseph Street. I started the engine, and a cop was standing nearby, who I didn't see. I quickly turned it off. The cop walked over to the car and he said, "Would you start up your car for me?"

After complying to his request, it was a deafening noise. He wrote out a citation that said I had forty-eight hours to get it fixed. The next day, at the smaller police station on Main Street at that time, I stopped the car about a half block from the station. After taking off in low gear about the time I was at the station, I let off the gas, and two police officers ran out of the station. They said, "Our coffee cups almost vibrated off the table," and after showing them my citation, I still had twenty-four hours to get it fixed.

The passenger side door never latched very well on the Ford. Wayne and I were coming back from Hot Springs; there was a hot mineral swimming pool there. We came back the scenic route through Custer State Park. Going around a curve too fast, the door came open. Wayne went out the door but managed to hold on to the top of the seat and the door handle. I drove out in the field and turned the car to the right, which allowed him to get back in the car. Driving back on to the road, I never did stop; we went on to town.

Normally in a public swimming pool, the kiddies' end of the pool is not much deeper than eighteen inches to two feet. Wayne dove off the top of the old original slide into the shallow end and swam through a hole in the kiddies' pool, out through another hole on the other side. The first time he did that, I could hardly believe it. It was nothing for people to dive off from the spectator seats into the water. That is why they put up a wire fence, as it is now.

When Sooper Dooper built a store toward Sturgis, a man in the meat department was from Germany; his sister had married a US Air Force man, that's how she got over here. They were about as compatible as a dog and a strange cat. I was transferred to the new store, and we ran the bars together a few years. He never did buy a car, which I never understood. One time, he drove a 1949 Ford like the one I owned, to the grocery store for me to try out. When I shifted from low to second gear, I must have done something wrong because Henry had to call the used car lot and tell them where their car was parked.

In the eleventh grade, I bought a 1946 Ford convertible. I used it mostly to drive girls to their boyfriends. I had come over to Casper to visit Dad, and on CY Street, I looked back to see if anyone was in the other lane, when my lane stopped. It was the first and only time the police had to be called, when I had a wreck while driving. The bill for the other car was not much more than $150, and about the only thing I did to my car was I broke the radiator. After going to a gas station, I put some Stop Leak in the radiator and on the way back to Rapid City, the radiator started leaking.

Not far from Douglas, which is fifty miles from Casper, Wyoming, I had parked the car on the highway. A farmer came over and said I could drive the car over to his yard, where no one would bother it. It was the farmer that I felt like was after my car, so I asked him if he had any gallon jugs to put water in. He gave me several, and I filled them up, and driving back to Rapid City, I broke the engine block. When I arrived in Rapid City, steam was coming out of the exhaust pipe. On the way there, I had stopped at every place I could to fill my jugs with water; even a mud hole wasn't beneath me. If the engine trouble wasn't enough, when I was driving down the highway, the hood flew up, but I could see a car coming between the car and the bottom of the hood, so I just kept on driving. I wanted to impress him.

One time, a car was coming on a two-lane road, and I drove all the way over past the white line on the left until he went by; that was another one that I impressed.

The 1946 Ford convertible, I never told Paul, but when I was working at the grocery store, it started to rain. I went out and started the engine to put the top up. I forgot to shut it off and left it running when I went back inside the store. It was hotter than a pistol by the time I got off work. At that time, the engines were air cooled which means the car needed to be driven to keep it cool.

Dad was telling the story at the coffee break to the other carpenters, and one of them said he had an engine that he could have for fifty dollars. Paul took the engine out and put the new one in, but it wasn't any better than the other one.

Paul was down at the Lincoln garage and saw a beautiful 1950 Lincoln on their lot. He drained all the water out and changed the oil of my beautiful white convertible, so they made the trade for the Lincoln. A girl drove the convertible off the lot to try it out, and she noticed the engine getting hot. She stopped at a gasoline service station and put water in the radiator, which was normal, but the dealership accused her for breaking the block.

Henry and I went to Deadwood to pay the prostitutes a visit in the Lincoln; the first trip was a textbook example of the way it should be done. I never knew it at the time, but she had set an alarm clock to go off in five minutes, the same time I went off. The town fathers eliminated the girls, and gambling has been the main source of income. The next time we went, the girls said we were too drunk, and they never had to set the alarm clock. On the way back to Rapid City, I was driving on solid ice. As I was coming around the corner, the Lincoln went sideways about a half of a block, bent over a post and slowly went into a ditch, back end first. Then it whipped around, curled up the front end, and the back window sailed about fifty feet and I was leaning up on the other side of a wire fence. Henry ended up in the back seat.

Walking toward Sturgis, we could hardly stand up on the ice. We hitchhiked to Rapid City, and Dad happened to be in town. I asked him if he would pull the Lincoln back to Ma's house. He got about a fifty-foot rope, and when we got to the car, he told henry that it looked like we had rolled it end over end. Henry said that is what we did, and he died believing that.

Dad tied the roper onto the car, and he sling-shot it out of the ditch. On the way toward Rapid City, he drove like we weren't attached to his truck. It was all my responsibility to keep the rope taut. We went through Sturgis, but I don't believe Dad noticed. When we got to Rapid City, Henry said that was the worst ride that he had ever been on.

Paul bought a 1950 Cosmopolitan Lincoln, which I paid for. It was bigger, but the motor was ruined, and he put the wrecked Lincoln motor in it.

I had gone to a bar with a band, and it wasn't long after I got there that they announced over the loudspeaker that a car was on fire outside. The second time, they said a Lincoln was on fire in the parking lot. That got my attention

70

and I went outside. The fire department had my back seat out of the car, dousing it with water. My cigarette ashes had blown back onto the back seat and had started the fire. I never did replace it; anyone that rode in the back seat had to sit on the floor.

It was this same Lincoln that I took rabbit hunting, and not far from town, I noticed the race track gate was left open. It went pretty well the first time around the track, so I decided to give it some gas. On the second turn, I spun around and the front end went into the bank; it broke the radiator, and antifreeze was leaking out on the ground. I called Paul on the phone and asked him if he would pull the car to Ma's house.

Each year, when I got a small tax refund from the government, I would usually have to spend it on a different car. The 1949 Ford was the fastest car in a block; it was seldom that I lost a race. That was usually how I tore the cars up.

Graduating from high school was not far away, and I told Mom that I have been going to school thirteen years, and I had never missed a day except a few sick days. I told her that today, I'm not going to school, I'm going rabbit hunting. Taking my .22 out to the car, I put it in the trunk. Three miles out highway 79, in my rearview mirror, I saw a cop car with his lights and is topped. He told me to get out and open the trunk, which I complied. I was wondering how they knew I wasn't going to attend school that day. Reaching in to take the .22 out, I told them I was going to go rabbit hunting. The cop told me to leave it alone. It turned out, a couple of men had escaped from jail, and one of the neighbors thought I was going to take them a gun.

One night, Henry and I was in the Seventh Avenue bar. A couple was fascinated that Henry was from Germany. We told them that I just got off the plane from there, and I never knew any English. They should have noticed that I never knew the German language either. They bought us so many drinks that Henry had to almost carry me out to the car. I took Henry home, and when I got to my house, I crawled on my hands and knees into the house.

We were in the same bar when Art wanted to fight Henry. We went outside, and Henry hit him with one punch that knocked him out. His head hit the edge of the curb; I thought he was going to bleed to death. At that time, he worked at a wild-game processing establishment, and he could take a deer from one fender, walk around, get the other deer, carry them in, and lay them on the meat block for processing. He never looked that big and strong, but he was.

One night, Henry took a girl to a family dance hall. When we left and got in the car, I asked Henry where he wanted to go. The girl said, "Take Henry home first." I had hardly said anything to her all night nor did we dance together. After Henry got out of the car, we parked nearby behind the grocery store.

The night of my graduation from Rapid City High School, Paul and Mom were the only ones on the audience on my behalf. I'm not sure where my guardian was.
Paul and I went to several bars where I met a new girl. When we left the bar and went out to the car, Paul asked me, "Where do you want to go?" I told him to take us to the Harney Hotel.

We went up to the room, and when we got there, it never took me very long to undress. The girl looked down and what I had, and she said, "It's too big," and ran out of the room. I walked home.

Years later, a girl told me, "You went where no one had ever gone before." That was unique.

One of the first things that Henry and I did after graduated from high school was we went to the horse track races in California. At the time, I had a1950 Buick that used about a quart of oil for every tank gas. In one of the magazines, I read that a person can make a living betting on the horses. It explained that if you bet on the favorites (which the professionals spend hours studying the program guide) they are right most of the time. "What you do," it said, "is bet on the favorites to show. If you lose, double up on your money in the next race. The three categories that you can bet on the horses are either win, place, or show," at that time. It all sounded logical to me. That was what my son told the girl on his first date when he took her home; everything we did was logical.

I didn't think the Buick would make the trips, so I told Henry when the car quits running, we will take a bus the rest of the way. In the middle of Wyoming, the alternator burned up, and at night, we turned the lights off to save the electrical charge in the battery. We started from Rapid City, about three p.m., and drove at night. When we arrived in Oakland, California, after giving up a few dollars gambling in Reno, Nevada, we had a decision to make and bought an alternator. The Buick was still running.

It was unbelievable, the small amount of money that a person won on a show ticket. If my horse never showed up, I had a lot of money to make up. The truth was, you had to quadruple your money on the next bet instead of doubling it. Nothing seemed to go very well; neither did the blackjack and keno in Reno, Nevada. At that time, the keno girls were cute as a June bug in May. Now, most of the guys are retired with gray hair.

The only thing that went right was the Buick; it never did quit. We arrived back in Rapid City broke with the realization that we were going to have to work for a living until we retired or got killed. The latter would have been the best option that would have bet on.

Chapter 8

CASPER, WYOMING

After graduation from high school, I moved to Casper, Wyoming, to live with Dad in his old green trailer that we had bought in Pierre, South Dakota, in 1949. I was back sleeping on the couch that made out into a bed in the front room. By this time, we made a good pair, with the drinking and etc. the trailer was heated from a fifty-five-gallon fuel oil barrel, and it was too much stove in BTUs for the trailer. When Dad would get up in the morning, he would open the front door because of too much heat. I was sleeping on the couch when he opened the door, and this time, it came back and slammed shut. My 1950 Lincoln's fender was about eighteen inches from the door, with just enough room to allow me to get in the door when I came home from the bar. Dad said, "You're going to have to get up and move your car."

In the morning, when I woke up on the bed, it was next to the furnace, and my head would be so hot, it felt like it was going to explode because of the heat.

One morning, Dad sat on, my feet with hid full body weight. If he told me to get up, I never heard him.

The first thing that I did was join the; labor union, and I went to work at the Alcova housing project near the dam. Dad and his brother Leroy were working there already.

The boss told me to transfer the gravel across the road with a wheelbarrow. I only weighed 125 pounds or less.

After three days went by, Dad saw that I just barely had a pulse. He talked the boss into letting me be a carpenter's helper. When the job was about finished and I was laid off, the business agent sent me to the Standard Oil Refinery in Casper. They were adding a new section; I believe they called it a waxing unit.

After a month or two of digging ditches, I heard that they needed someone to work in the office. With a 25 percent pay cut per hour, I moved in the office as a field time keeper for Foster and Wheeler Construction Company. It consisted of keeping track of each man's job and the time it took him to do it. If they were doing something that required more pay, I had to keep track of that. A couple of men before me had tried out for the job and failed. I never saw anything hard about it; each job had a number. The company used the information to bid on a similar project in the future.

We lived at the Riverside Trailer Court in the small 8x29 foot trailer. On Saturday night, they had a dance with live music in a small building nearby. The night I met Blondie, I'm not sure where her husband was, probably at home taking care of her five children. She had just returned from Texas, after leaving Casper with another man. We went to the trailer, she seduced me, and it happened often after that. One day, we drove out of town in her car and parked near the highway on 1-25 north. I'm not sure why she wanted me to drive the car back to the trailer court, where we both lived, but she did.

Driving around a corner, standing in the road was her husband, at least six feet tall and weighing a measly two hundred fifty pounds. I almost died. Stopping the car, I got out he pushed me away from the car, got in, and drove off. I was happy that I didn't have to do anything radical to him. We only got it together one more time after that. Her upper plate fell out when I turned her over, and that was embarrassing for her. She must have impressed Dad. He asked me forty years later if I still saw Blondie.

One time, I think Dad should have stayed in bed. When he got up, he told his girlfriend, "It is either me or the dogs."

I'm not sure what Dad was doing in a bar in Glenrock, thirty miles from Casper. He met a homeless couple, and he told them they could come home with him. He only had a double bed, so the three of them slept in it with the wife in the middle. The next day, they went somewhere and got their daughter. The only place left to sleep was with me; the couch had double-sized bed inside it. A few days later, Dad told me that if I wanted to marry their daughter, I could have the trailer.

In the morning, the husband's hands shook so much, he couldn't get the shot glass of whiskey to his mouth. The wife had to feed the first three glasses to him, and the rest of the day, he was okay until the next morning.

Thanksgiving came, and Dad cooked a typical dinner of turkey, mashed potatoes, dressing with oysters, cranberries, cream-style corn, etc. the next morning, someone had removed one of the turkey legs and ate it. The rest of the meal was the way Dad had put it on the table.

After Thanksgiving, they told us they found a trailer to rent in the same trailer court. Her husband never said it, but I'm sure that while they were living there, he felt hoodwinked. I believe she thought of it as paying dues.

Dad started going with a rough-and-ready woman named Jesse. She said she had as much sex with different men as the spines that stuck out of porcupine. When Dad bought a half pint of whiskey, she would drink a good part of it, Dad would finish it off and throw the bottle out the window, if we were in the car. She had a daughter that wasn't as crusty, who slept with me a few nights.

After they found love someplace else, Dad met another woman with ten children. Her sister was married to a man in Nebraska, and she came to Casper for vacation. She was going to stay one week, and she seduced me for two weeks. It was the second Saturday that we got into an argument, and I went drinking and dancing by myself. Dad took both of the girls out to party, and I had just arrived home when I heard them come in the front door. Dad said, "Mickey's mad at you. Why don't you come back and sleep with us?"

His girlfriend kept one eye open. I'm not sure how long we were snuggled up in the two beds (when Dad told me the next morning), then the husband from Nebraska came barging through the front door, with a loaded .22 rifle. He saw me sleeping by myself in the front room, and now Dad had some explaining to do. I was passed out or asleep throughout the entire ordeal. Her husband got one of the kids to take him to the trailer. No one was shot, and he took her back to Nebraska slightly used.

When Dad was laid off of the job at Alcova, he went to work at the Standard Oil Refinery for Foster Wheeler. He was laid off first, and he asked me if I had thirty dollars for gas. He was going to Idaho Falls, Idaho. I gave him the money, but now I had to rent a place to live.

The first mistake I made after I rented an apartment was I started running around with a crazy guy, and when I went to bed, he had to leave, but all the girls could stay. A word that you seldom hear anymore is what he was mixed up with, and that was statutory rape. That is when a girl is under the legal age of consent, and that happened before I met him.

With Dad out of the picture, I had met a girl that never drank, and we had gone up on Casper Mountain to have a picnic. Because she never drank, I had only couple of beers. When I took her home, as I was backing out from her place on Collins Street, my front bumper hooked a guide wire that was connected from the top of a pole to the ground.

A cop drove up. I went over where he parked and asked him if he had a flashlight. He smelled the beer on my breath and arrested me for drunken driving. It made me mad, so I hired an attorney that got the case thrown out of court. When I went into the drunk tank, three or four men were asleep on the floor, but there was one cot that was empty. It was the one that I wanted. The next morning, we got two boiled eggs for breakfast, and one of the old salts told me that I had better save one of them in case I got hungry.

After breakfast, a bail bondsman was outside the cage and asked if anyone wanted to be bonded out. I raised my hand, and one of the prisoners said, "You mean, you have money?"

It felt like the shower couldn't get my body clean when getting out. It was the first time and last time that I was ever arrested for drunken driving. I was good at passing the police tests. During that period, they never had breath analysis or blood tests as they do now.

My life was like that song Willy Nelson sand: all the girls I met before were coming in and out my door. I never had any standards; only one had nipples so far from her body that it embarrassed me when we went in a café.

One girl had to have a pizza every day, and in a few days, I traded her in for her girlfriend. Her name was Tommy Joe, and her life's ambition was to go to Deadwood, South Dakota, and become a prostitute. I'm not sure if she ever achieved her life's goal or not.

There was a seedy hotel, I believe the name of it was Collins Hotel, across from the Bi-Right Drug Store. We had been out drinking, and she took me to her house, if you could call it that; it had since been torn down. During the night, both of us fell off the bed, and the next morning when I woke up, I was in bed by myself. I remembered that I was with Tommy Joe, and both of us fell off the bed. Looking under the bed, she was sound asleep in filth that had been there since the building was constructed, probably 1900.

My 1950 Lincoln developed a problem with the transmission. One of the guys that I worked with was picking me up and taking me home. I never had a perfect attendance record, but they never fired me. If they walked in my shoes, it would have given them some insight on the cause.

There was a knock on the door, and my crazy friend had found two new girls. They had an old car, and they wanted to get some beer and ride around. They took me to a bar in Mills. I purchased two six-packs. Riding around awhile, the girls said they wanted to go home. When they drove to their house, my crazy friend said, "Can I borrow your car?"

The girl loaned him the car, and we went to the same place to get another six-pack of beer. I had steered him back on the road a couple times, and he turned down the road past the Wagon Wheel Roller Skating Rink. Before that, it was a family dance hall; what that meant was you had to keep your bottle out in the car.

About a mile down the road, there was a railroad track that was higher than the pavement. He was driving on the wrong side of the road and hit the other car in a head-on collision. The report said he knocked the other car backward eleven feet on impact. When the ambulance came, I was lying on the front fender. I had gone through the windshield and had just put the can of beer to my mouth on impact. That probably broke the windshield. When I woke up the next day, about ten a.m., a man from the insurance company was there, and he said, "If you sign these papers, we won't bring a lawsuit against you." I signed the papers.

The crazy was in the next bed with a cut on his nose. Outside of rearranging my face, I broke the mandible in my right jaw. At that time, they couldn't repair it, and on the second operation, it was removed. When I saw the doctor the first time, I asked him if he used any anesthetic on my face when the stitched me up. He said, "You had enough in you and never needed any."

Paul came to see me first, and my injuries affected him more than it did me. After he left the hospital, he said that he quit speeding. Mom brought me a pair of trousers, and I wept. A pink lady volunteer told me that I had ruined my life. Just before I got out of the hospital, Dad drove from Idaho Falls, Idaho. We went out in the hall and sat in a love seat where he went to sleep. That evening, he brought all the people from the bar to see me, and it raised my temperature; that made the hospital concerned.

I was in the hospital twenty-one days, and the last night, there was a severe accident about fifty miles from Casper: five high school kids in a car. Only two out of five were alive. They put one of them in my room. Family members or friends were coming in the room, looking to see which one was alive.

I went to the nurse's station and asked them for a sleeping pill; it kept me awake about thirty days. In the morning, the police came and escorted me to the police station, where I told them where I bought the beer. In Wyoming, you had to be twenty-one; I was nineteen years old. The accident happened a year after graduating from high school.

In the apartment where I was living, the owner told me that I had one too many parties and that I had to leave. I rented a one bedroom/bath studio apartment, and they told me that I couldn't have any girlfriends in my room.

Tommy Joe, her friend, and I were out partying. We couldn't find her friend's boyfriend. Tommy Joe told her, "Why don't you sleep with us?"

We went to my house, and I took them around the back to a tree. I told them, I'll go upstairs, and open the window up there, and you will have to climb up the tree."

It wasn't long until both of them were in the bed with me, which was the first and only time I ever slept with two girls at the same time. My girlfriend told me sometime in the night that it was all right with her if I moved over on the other side of the bed.

The girls never knew that Paul came to take me back home when he came the next day, but we had to have one last fling. The friend went with Paul. After he achieved his goal when the sun was coming up, he told me afterward that she said, "Let's do it again." It took him so long in the fight the first time that he was tuckered out.

The next day, Paul and I went back to Rapid City, South Dakota. Mom was probably delighted.

Foster and Wheeler Construction Company was going to take me with them to Missouri to another job when they were finished in Casper, but the accident ended that plan.

Chapter 9

RAPID CITY: THE SECOND TIME

In Rapid City, I told Mom that I had black specks floating around in my eye. She made an appointment with an optometrist, and he gave me a prescription to fill at the drug store, then he made me another appointment. I told Paul that evening, and the next day, he took me out to the Air Force Base for an examination. The optometrist out there said that I scarred my eyeball from glass in the car wreck, and there was nothing that could be done. I cancelled my appointment with the optometrist in Rapid City and never filled my prescription.

I had met a girl on one of my trips visiting Mom and went with her a few times. After the car wreck, I went to her house and told her I was in a bad car accident and that I wouldn't be seeing her anymore. My face was mess. I thought, at the time, that the girls that I went with from now on could reject me or accept me with my new face.

After signing up for unemployment insurance in Rapid City on Wyoming, Sooper Dooper wanted me to go back to work for them, but I would have to take a pay cut. Eventually, I went back and worked for them two or three more years.

One day, Dad was back in town in Rapid City, and he had run into Linda, his second wife from Canada, at the bar. When they lived together in Casper, she had run off with another man, but now she wanted to come back to him. He asked me if I would go to Casper and tell the woman that he had brought from Idaho to leave.

When arriving at the trailer, I went to bed in the front room, deciding to tell her in the morning, but I changed my mind and decided to get it over with. When I called her name to see if she was awake, she said yes, and when I went to the bed at the back of the trailer, she was taking off her panties, so I decided I would tell her in the morning. The next morning, when I told her that she had to leave, she wouldn't go and moved into another trailer close by with another man. When Dad arrived, he put her on a bus for Idaho Falls, Idaho, with Linda present. He married three women with one divorce.

Before I left Rapid City, I had a full-blown case of the crabs. She took them back to Idaho, and I gave them one to one of my old flames before I knew what I had crawling on me. They even took up residence under my arm.

One night at a dance, I met Muriel. She was an Indian girl with three children. She worked nights from ten p.m. at the bakery next to the movie theater. We had a favorite spot in rock quarry to park; because of her kids before, she had this thing about not removing her panties. On a weekend at her house, she never had any problem with it. I had to pull the elastic of her panties to the side with one hand; it was as if it was gift wrapped all the time, which I didn't mind. When she got to work, she always complained about the liquid running down her legs, and I'm not sure if it ever got to her shoe or not.

With her going to work at ten p.m. that left me time for my other endeavors or indulgences.

There were three of us guys parked in a car on Main Street in Rapid City. The one in the center was more knowledgeable than Henry and I he said, "What they are doing now is licking the jar, but they are pouring wine on it first."

The next weekend, when it was going hot ns heavy with Muriel at her house, the only thing that I had was whiskey. I found out that wasn't a good idea. She blooded my nose. Have you ever been hit in the face with a cat?

It was almost routine that whatever time I came home, I would get myself something to eat, and I never turned the light on. Making a salami sandwich one night, I ate at least half of it, but I noticed it was tough chewing and left it on the table. When I got up, I looked at the sandwich and half of the cardboard was gone. At that time, on the bottom of a package of lunch meat, they placed a cardboard and stacked the lunch meat on top of it before they wrapped it.

One day, I was drunk—I wish I could say that some other way—driving on Seventh or Eighth Street. I stopped the car; an Indian girl got in that I had never met before, and she said that she was going to a party. I drove to a liquor store and bought a pint of whiskey. When I came out of the store, I noticed a flat tire on the car. The party sounded better to me than fixing the flat, so I drove to the party with the flat. That was before steel-belted tires, and when I said flat, it was flat. When we arrived at the party, we went to the bedroom that wasn't being used. As we were making love, her friends started coming in for a drink out of my

86

bottle. I poured them a drink in their water glass, and I have heard of girls eating pudding out of a bowl.

At the grocery store, I was third in line from manager, so each of us took turns being the manager on weekends and at night until closing. The last thing we did was clear the three machines of the day's receipts, put the proceeds in a money bag, and take it to the police station.

One night, I threw the money bag behind the seat and went to the bar. The next morning, I saw the money bag behind the back seat. I was wondering if the police were looking for me. Taking the money to the police station, as I was leaving, the main boss that usually picked it up each morning was driving in the entry as I was driving out the exit. The boss had a small surplus of money in the bar. I went to the store and took $5 or $10 to tide me over. Sometimes I left an IOU slip, and they would take it out of my next paycheck.

My salary doubled from $125 to $250 a month in six years. I guess I took after Dad; I couldn't stand prosperity, so I quit the store the second time.

The next job that I had was at Earl's Poultry Market candling eggs. That consisted of holding two eggs in each hand and bringing them to a lighted hole of a box to check their condition. It was Earl's job to drive to the different farms and collect the eggs. In about a year, he bought some eggs that weren't grade A, but I tried to make do by cheating on the quality. He received too many complaints and told me that he was going to get along without me. The girl candling eggs next to me was my main distraction.

There was an advertisement in the Help Wanted section of the newspaper that said they wanted someone to work at Rushmore Bakery. It consisted of loading the individual bakery trucks for their different routes around town. Every day, they drivers would give me a list of what they needed. The bakers had already received it to bake the right amount of bread and sweet rolls. When I was finished with that, I helped the man on a machine wrap the bread in cellophane tightly. It wasn't a good way to preserve the bread; when a person opened the loaf, half of it would dry out.

One day, out of the blue, Mom asked me, "Why don't you go into the air force?"

The way it was going, my life never looked very promising, so I surprised her by saying the next day, "I would join the navy."

The hardest part was telling Henry what I was going to do. He hated the military with a passion because of World War II, Hitler dragging Germany into the war. So many men, women, and children were killed on both sides with the slaughter of the Jews, etc. he was drafted into the US army but couldn't speak any English, so they sent him back home.

In 1599, I went down to the navy recruiter at the courthouse and started the enlistment procedure. I'm not sure why I picked the navy. I got so carsick when I was a child. I was twenty-two years old. Most of the people that go into military go in after they graduate from high school; they are usually seventeen or eighteen years old.

The morning that I was going to legally join up by raising my hand, my witness was an FBI agent that had an office in the building. He seemed to know about the wild and crazy life I was leading; he was the happiest man in the room. When I signed the papers, I told the recruiter that I just received a penicillin shot for gonorrhea. He said, "You'll fit right in."

At that time, syphilis was the venereal disease that was the worst thing one could acquire, and HIV or AIDS was not a factor for the promiscuous.

Chapter 10

US NAVY

The first time that I had ever flown in an air plane was from Rapid City, South Dakota, to San Diego, California, where I was going for basic training.

Before the plane got off the ground, Mom threw everything I owned out in the trash. She gave me my .22 rifle away to Merlyn, my sister's husband. A lot of the things that I had would have been valuable today: comic books, toys, white gold pocket watch, etc. I don't blame her because ever since her divorce from Dad, I put every gray hair on her head. If I would have come back as a failure on the Navy, I'm not sure if she would have let me in the house or not. I don't think so.

In the airplane, my ears couldn't adjust to the air pressure. I thought my head was going to explode. This was something that I figured out many years later, the cause of this, which is almost unbelievable, but I'll give it my best. On the farm I played hard, and if my teeth were half black when I was eleven by the time we got to Rapid City, what about the inside of my ears? Both of them were full of dirt and wax. That is why I couldn't pass the hearing tests in the school very well.

In boot training, they had a hearing test, but all I had to do was repeat what a man said back to him. No one ever looked in my ears. I was assigned to the main engine room of LSD3 (landing ship dock). In the main engine room, we gave the orders instead of taking them. That way, I never had to hear all that well. However, I did it; I managed to get through eight years in the navy. I was years later than I found out what my problem had been. Some of the women might have asked me to marry them, but I couldn't hear ém.

The first day in boot training, our non-commissioned officer had us standing in rows. He wasn't very tall, but he said, "Is there anyone here that believes they can kick my ass? Step forward." No one made a move.

He turned out to be one of the nicest commanders that a person would get under those circumstances. Our sister company, it wasn't so much the commander as it was the people he put in charge when he wasn't there that was the problem.

Our company never got the duty of the mess hall (where we ate), and that turned out well. We had other jobs on the base.

I never had one discrepancy until one day at our morning inspection. The inspecting officer noticed that my leggings were not laced right. My punishment was to wash all the leggings for the entire company of thirty men.

There was a couple of guys that wouldn't take a bath. They got washed down with a scrub and sent to a special company before they were sent back home to their mother. A few would manage to be sent back to a regular company, but not very many.

About a month before we graduated, we were sent on liberty to San Diego, the deserving, and I knew how to party. When I got off the bus around midnight, I was almost run over on the highway at the gate. The keepers of the gate made me stay in their shack until I proved I could go to my barracks. After graduating from boot training, I went to a receiving station to wait for orders to my duty station. At the receiving station, they told me one morning to report to the mess hall. When I got there, they took me in the scullery and told me to wash the pots and pans. They were stacked up almost to the ceiling, about sixteen feet long. As I was filling the sink, a sailor came to the door, and I heard my name, Mullen. I said yes; he told me to come with him. He took me to another room and cut up about three pounds of lunch meat with a meat slicer. He told me to wrap it up with white freezer paper, clean the slicer, and wipe up around the area.

That was all I had to do the rest of the day. There is a God.

When the orders arrived, three of us would go to Hawaii for about six months of temporary duty. From San Diego to Hawaii, my transportation was on an LST (landing ship tank). It only went about nine miles an hour. They picked me and two others to stand watch on some vehicles strapped down on a deck inside the ship, four hours on, eight off. Before they put the vehicles on the deck, they opened up some tanks underneath them to spray a preservative inside. During that process, the hose broke, and the preservative went all over the deck. I got so seasick that I thought I was going to die. When I went up to eat, the chow line formed outside where the diesel exhaust came out from the engine.

On the ship that I was assigned to, someone told me that sick bay had a pill to prevent seasickness. To my knowledge, the pill was never mentioned in boot training. It took about twenty days to get to Hawaii, and when the ship was going up the harbor past the ships that were sunk during World War II by the Japanese, I thought this must be what heaven feels like. The air force even sounded good that Mom mentioned in the first place.

I never had a clue how I was going to stay in the Navy, thinking that I was going to be sick the rest of the enlistment, over three years to go. At my duty station in Hawaii, I tried to get out of the navy on a physical discharge. I should have come right out and told them what my problem was getting seasick. They would have handed me a pill, and that would have been the end of it. I called them my pregnant pills because that was what I was told they were for, morning sickness that women had when they are pregnant. They assigned me to the automotive garage, which was about as good of duty as I could hope for. The navy hired a civilian mechanic to work on the cars, so all I had to do was keep the place clean and wash the captain's car.

The garbage dump caught on fire the morning they were going to have an inspection: the mother of them all, personnel, barracks, and grounds, etc.

They assigned me to put the fire out with a civilian driving the fire truck. I never wanted to rush into it, so every half hour, I squirted a little water on it create a little smoke. When the inspection was over and everybody was dismissed to go on liberty to Honolulu, the fire by this time was difficult to put out. It had crept further down in the pile, but eventually, I got it out and went to town a little late. I sued a forklift for transportation a couple of weeks to go to chow, etc., until they took the key away from me.

In three months, they had a shortage of help in the mess hall, and I was transferred there. At first, I was the salad girl; on the mess deck, that was about as good as it could get. In Hawaii, there was no shortage of fruit and vegetables for the different salads that I made.

There was only one problem. The bus schedule wasn't even close to the hours that we worked. The bus went to Schofield Army Base, then we h ad to ride a city bus to Honolulu. I told two of the other mess hands that what we needed was a car. I had already stopped with a wild pig strapped to each of his front fenders of a Jeep. The navy told me I would see the world, but all I could see was two pigs' rear ends. As far as I know, wild pig hunting is all there is in Hawaii.

The sailor from Mississippi who wore his first pair of shoes when he joined the navy said, "I'll do it. Get us a car."

We took up a collection, the way Dad did when he was the preacher. I'm not sure where he got the car, but it wouldn't start unless you pushed it, jumped in, put it in gear, and popped (let out) the clutch. With a liberty card in your back pocket, that produced some adrenaline. Starting the car wasn't too much a kid when he saved gas coasting down the hills.

Just before we got the wheels. I was down on hotel Street in Honolulu at a bar and dance hall. I asked a Philippine girl if she wanted to dance; women were few and far between. I hadn't had any luck, and I had been there three months. I asked Puka Puka, the auto mechanic, what the problem was. He said that it all started in World War II, when the soldiers never treated the native girls very well. There was a documentary about that on TV not long ago. It showed men in lines that went around the block. At the head of the line would be a girl charging three dollars for three minutes. In Deadwood, South Dakota, at least you got five minutes. There was a crisis; they wanted to charge five dollars, and the US government said no. the girls rebelled, and one of them said okay. In one room, we will have the sailor remove his clothes. In the next room, we will give him the three minutes of service, and in the third room, he can put his uniform back on. It was a fast-track production line that made as much money for the girls as charging five dollars.

The Philippine girl got up to dance, and it was all downhill from there. I told her that the next time she saw me, I would have a car, but tonight, we would get a cab. We had the cab driver go to a few hotels that I could afford, and they were all full.

With the two of us in the back seat, I asked the cab driver if he needed a cup of coffee. He parked behind a café and went in. She jumped on my bones, and when he came back out, about a half hour later, I told him to take me to the bus stop.

Missing the bus at the army base to my duty station, I started walking toward the base, arriving about the time the sun came up, but no one ever did. I'm not sure what I was stepping on that was on the road. It was some kind of animal. It was so dark, I couldn't see what it was. If I had to guess, I would say it was some king of lizard.

95

The next time that we had a date, I had the car like I said I would. A few dates later came the question, "Why do you park the car on a hill?"

I told her, "It's easier to start the car."

In the mess decks, another problem came up. The guy they had put in the scullery was not only making a physical but mental mess out of washing the dishes. At times, he would stand and cry when too many dishes would pile up at the window. One of the cooks never liked him at all, and there was a dark area near the mess deck. One night, he hit him over the head with a sock with a bar of soap in it. He told me that the soap wouldn't fracture his skull. The commander of the base found out who did it, and the cook was restricted to the base. At the captain's mast, the captain said the kid deserved it, but it was against navy regulations to put a bar of soap in a sock and use it like he did. When I received my orders to go to a ship, I was told the kid had orders to go to Annapolis Navy College. He had an extremely high score on one of the written tests that we both took.

The boss put me in the scullery, and with a little organization, it was another dream job. I would get done before anyone else and get to the car, going to Honolulu before the others would get finished with their work.

One day, I got the phone call I was waiting for. "I'm pregnant."

We ended up getting married by a court judge in Honolulu, the judge said we had to have a witness, and a woman out on the street said she would be out witness. We used the same ring that she was given for her first marriage. When I arrived in Honolulu, it was three months before I got lucky, and I never wanted to go through that again.

One time, the co-owner and I parked the car to go shopping in Honolulu without any money. On the way back to the car, I said, "that looks like our car on the back of that wrecker."

He said, "No it couldn't be."

We got to the spot where we had parked and there was a sign: no parking between the hours: Monday, Wednesday, and Friday.

He said, "That was our car."

Between the three of us that bought the car, with no insurance, we managed to accumulate thirteen tickets. I don't remember getting a driver's license, but I must have had one. They might have had a rule that you could use your license from whatever state you were from. The navy commander of the base went out and pulled the wiring out from under the dash, disabling the car.

Not long after we lost the car, my orders came in, and they wanted me stationed on the USS Carter Hall LSD 3 to keep me out of trouble.

Chapter 11

USS CARTER HALL
LSD 3

There were three of us riding a train through japan, going to Sasebo where the ship docked. We were drinking beer along the way, and I said, "This was not like Casper, Wyoming."

One of the guys said, "Casper, that is where I'm from."

I said I lived in the Riverside Trailer Court, and he said he did too. When he was stationed in Hawaii, he had cut his foot on coral, and to my knowledge, it never healed. One day on the ship, a guy told me that he was discharged for too many traffic tickets. The train arrived in Sasebo, and the ship returned from Korea. I'm not sure when I was designated to be a machinist's mate, but I found myself in the main engine room as my cleaning station. That was about all I did for the first four years: wash, chip, or paint. The salt air was so bad on the bare metal, you could watch it rust.

The ship was a dinosaur; the two main engines were similar to the ones that were used on the trains during the Plains Indian Wars. The steam engine had five reciprocating pistons, about twenty-eight inches in diameter, with huge counterweights. They had to have a certain amount of oil to make them work. The oil was a detriment to the water, where the boiler got its water. Ninety percent of the steam used went back into the hot well as water for the boiler to make more steam. There were two drums with a few layers of filters that was surged with, I believe, asbestos to remove the oil from the feed water. If it got too much oil in the water, we pumped a slurry of asbestos in to the filters to clear it up.

The main engineer was a warrant officer, who told me his first ship was on a sailing vessel. We got along well. I think he could spot an engineer from across the room.

When going on liberty in Sasebo, the closest bar was my first stop. I sat down in a booth, and it wasn't long until one of the Japanese girls came over and sat down next to me. It never took me all day to fall in love. After a few drinks, with her drinking something that would resemble Kool-Aid, she said that if I gave the bartender some money, she could leave the bar. She took me to her house that was shared with another family. They used the same kitchen, and if I remember right, the bathroom was outside, above a benjo ditch. It would be about the same as the outhouse that I was familiar with. Everybody went to the same bathhouse in the neighborhood. It wouldn't surprise me none if the men and women bathed together. When we got to her house, she wanted some more money for herself. That's when I found out it wasn't about love; it was all about the money.

The next day, we went to a movie, and she stayed home from the bar. I accidentally touched her breast, reaching for the popcorn, and she said, "Do you want to go to my house?" it was the first time that I received the whole enchilada. Neither ship ever got back to Sasebo, so she had to find somebody else to entertain.

With the wife in Hawaii, I wrote her that when I got to Long Beach, I would rent an apartment and send for her. She was reluctant to leave Hawaii, and for a while, it was doubtful if she was going to come to California. She had to leave her little girl, three years old, and a son, about five. When she got a divorce, her husband got custody of the two children.

On day, she was there, and the apartment had a Murphy bed that dropped down out of the wall. The commissary was not far away by bus. I bought two six-packs of beer and a pound of hamburger with buns. For at least a year after she arrived in California, she threatened to go back to Hawaii.

When the ship left Long Beach, it went to Seattle, Washington, for a major overhaul at the shipyard. The first night I had the duty, the next night I went to a bar and dance hall. The girl that I met, she took me to her house, but it wasn't all it was cracked up to be. She needed an operation for expansion. The first night, my boss had bought her a few drinks, which I never knew anything about. When the boss went back to take up where he left off, she told him that "Mickey and I are going steady." When I got back to the ship, he accused me of taking his girl away from him.

One time, we were going to have an inspection of the engine room, he kicked me in the rear end when I was wire-brushing the deck on my hands and knees. If she stayed with him, she probably wouldn't need an operation, and I partied with her until the ship left.

One of her friends had a baby, and she never washed the kid's diaper, which at that time were cloth. Her friend threw them in the corner of the bathroom whey they were soiled. When the bus dropped me off at the corner, I could smell the house. No one had to ask her where the bathroom was.

Another of her friends was married, and her husband paid all the expenses for her and her boyfriend. They all slept in the same bed. In Seattle was the only place that I drank what we called moose milk; that was whisky and milk in a water glass. That was some potent drink because it was so mild.

In case I couldn't find tight lips, there was a spare that loved me. It was on one of those occasions that I woke up one morning in her bed. She had risen during the night, went sandwich, and took one bite out of it. The second bite, which was next to the first, she fell asleep, and that was the view I had the morning when I woke up. She had a baloney sandwich hanging out of her mouth.

After the shipyard got through with the ship, they tool it up a freshwater river to Spokane, Washington, for its shakedown cruise to find out if there was something wrong with it.

In Spokane, I happened upon a hot tamale that took longer than I liked to get her home. She finally ran out of gas about three a.m., and when I woke up the next morning, I only had twenty minutes to get to the ship in her car. Looking down at her in what she was born with, asleep, I told myself it was going to be impossible getting her up, but to my surprise, I was at the front gate of the base in about fifteen minutes. I told the marine that I had to get to

101

the ship, as I was running late, and would he let her drive mw to the ship. He motioned us through,
and after I was aboard, they untied the ship from the pier to go back to Seattle. They probably waited for me.

When the ship went back to Long Beach, California, it as one time that I was afraid to look out on the pier, because Seattle, Washington, wasn't very far from Long Beach, California, and I was engaged to be married. One time, in our apartment in Long Beach, I drank a little too much and was nauseated. I had my head down inside the commode with the seat up. The wife came in and asked me what I was doing. I said, "I'm washing my face." Another time, I lowered the white oven door of the cook stove in the kitchen and was nauseous in the oven. After all, it was white and it had some moving parts.

Up to this time, I stood messenger watches in the engine room, and we were going overseas. The messenger had to write down different temperatures of gages, make coffee, which was the first thing, sweep up at the end of the watch, and go wake up the people for the next watch.

I'm not sure who made up the watch list for the overseas trip we were about to go on, but he put me down for the throttles. The only thing that I knew about the throttles was the paperwork. I had never done the throttle part. There were two levers attached to the main engine: one of them was the lever to go forward and the other was to go backward. That was about all I knew.

One if the other sailors was on watch when we left and another when we got to Hawaii. We left Hawaii with another experienced sailor, and when we got to Okinawa, he was on watch when we anchored out. I was lucky again when we left Okinawa and went to Japan; my luck was still holding on.

In Japan, I learned how to do the lever part. I don't think it would have been good if we had an emergency out at sea. It would have sucked the steam out of the boiler if I never slowed the engine down with the throttle levers because the boiler room got the same signal from the officer on the bridge as we did in the engine room. There is an old saying, "It's better to be lucky than good."

In Okinawa, a girl that took me home with her had every appliance imaginable, but her house was not hooked up with electricity. I mentioned it to her, and she said it will come, and when it does, she's ready.

On the way back from Japan, we stopped in Hawaii, and I started drinking on Friday at noon. On Saturday, I thought I had the duty Sunday, so I went back to the ship to be at quarters Sunday morning. Standing in the hot sun at the morning muster, I fainted. They got a stretcher and took me to sick bay. My boss came in to see me, and I told him I was okay; that all I needed was a drink. My problem was my liberty card was in the box. I thought I had the duty, and that was the reason I came back to the ship. He got my liberty card, and I went back to Honolulu. Monday morning, hitchhiking back to the ship, a man stopped and picked me up. He hit me over the head with a blackjack and pushed me out the passenger door with his feet, grabbing my billfold. I was going back to the ship; the only time I had any money was going away. Without car, there was nothing in the billfold: driver's license, insurance card, credit cards, nothing. If he needed a billfold, I would have given it to him if he asked me. I'm not sure what he did with the picture of the wife.

When we got back to Long Beach, the wife said she was due to have the baby, and I called a cab. We went to the hospital. I had hardly got to sit down when the nurse handed me a baby boy. There was another man that had been in the waiting room all night. Removing the money from her purse, I went to the bar. I--t wasn't until five days later than I signed the papers to take her home. I could have taken her out about three days before. When she went home, she was fully capable of taking care of the baby, and I can't remember changing a diaper.

The ship went back overseas, and when we got back, it was put in a shipyard for a few repairs. We were going to be there for a while, but the captain got a message that we were to put the ship together. We were going to Cuba, the missile crisis with Russia. We were part of the fast task force; on a good day, we could do eighteen knots, about nineteen miles an hour.

We went in circles until the ship pulled into Jamaica, and the bosses-that-be put me on shore patrol. At the station where we received our instructions from the local shore patrol, one of the sailors asked the man, "Why do the marines get a hard hat and we don't"

He said, "You don't need any."

My assignment was in a bar, and in all my travels, I never saw anything like it. The tables were on a small pedestal located in the center. It was almost impossible to walk by them without everything on the table going off on the floor. By midnight, glass was about all you could walk on.

The girls in the bar took those that were "inclined" upstairs. I asked one of the girls, "How come they charge so much?"

She told me that it was like "removing a piece of their soul every time they made love."

When the crisis was over, on the way back to Long Beach, they stopped in Panama where I was turned loose, and it wasn't pretty. It's one of the few times that I don't remember much about the trip from town; all I can say is I left Panama on the ship. Going through the Panama Canal was interesting.

When I got back home, the wife had every container in the house filled with water; that is what they told people to do on TV.

Another shipmate, Lee, and I, at the time, were the only two on the ship that knew how to make unsalted water with the steam evaporator. When I relieved him for the next watch, he was running almost pure salt into the freshwater tank, trying to make more water per hour than me. I left it that way a couple hours and straightened the evaporator up to make good water. When Lee received me, I drank some of the water topside, and there was no doubt in my mind that both of us were going to walk the plank as the pirates did in their day. Surprisingly, no one ever said anything about the salt in the freshwater. Lee considered himself a con man, at least that is what he told Lee, "I'll go upstairs to make sure the girl is ready." That was the last time that he ever saw his twenty dollars.

The bowl that we used to test the water with chemicals had gotten broken in a storm. The boss said to use a coffee cup to test the water. It wasn't long until, absentmindedly, I drank from the coffee cup with the full assortment of chemicals. Is it any wonder that I have a problem with acid reflux disease in my stomach?

The ship went to a shipyard in San Francisco, and as a favor to the crew, the captain said he would load our cars on the top deck to take there. I never owned a car and was standing by the rail watching them take the cars off the ship. One of the sailors said, "That's my car."

He asked me if I wanted to go to San Francisco with him. It wasn't like me to miss an opportunity. I'm not sure how it happened, but we ended up in Oakland and after a few too many drinks, we decided to go back to San Francisco. Halfway across the bay bridge, a Volkswagen had run out of gas, with four people in the car. My escort ran into the rear end of the VW, and I had already heard of the law in California that the person over twenty-one years of age was responsible for the accident I said, "I think I'll go back to the ship now."

As I was walking toward San Francisco on the Oakland Bay Bridge in my way navy uniform, a car stopped. I got in the back seat. The lady asked me if I saw the wreck back there. I said, "Yes, that was a bad one," and would they let me out at the end of the bridge? They let me out, and I made it somehow back to the ship. A few days later, the men from the justice department came to the ship to talk to me. The division officer told them that I never had anything to do with the accident and they left.

I tried to rent a house for the wife but never had any luck, and found out that on the base, not far from the ship in dry dock, the navy rented a house for sailors. After we moved in, Dad drove from Casper, Wyoming for a visit but cut the visit short. The second day, he said he was going back to Casper and that it was too cold here for him.

It was in San Francisco that I made third class machinist's mate, and because I was so close to the ship, I told anyone that made an increase in rank that I had beer at my house. The ship captain heard about it. They decided to rent a facility for food and drink for a celebration; that was nice of them.

We made one trip to Thailand, where the military had taken some either outdated or damaged equipment from Vietnam for us to load up on our ship. I was sitting in a bar and the sun was shining through the back door, when it suddenly went dark.

The girl sitting at the table said, "Here comes my boyfriend."

He was a big merchant mariner that was big enough to shut the lights out without turning the switch off. I went to another bar. In that bar there was a girl that lived on a small boat in the harbor. I found out you can rock the boat. Others had brought girls out to the ship, so I told her to come out in the water taxi. The ship left that morning, and I saw her in a boat coming toward the ship as we passed by.

When I was honorably discharged as an enlisted man second class or E-5, the wife was working at the Fishermen Wharf in Long Beach, and because we were short of money, she brought home leftover Chinese food. It gave me a migraine headache, the only one that I had ever had in my life.

Before I was discharged from the navy, I was studying real estate salesman. For a little piece and quiet, I found a woman that worked days. I went over to her trailer to study while she was at work. She seduced me after she came home. We did the wash, rinse, and dry positions, starting from the bottom up, then I went home.

My first experience of door to door selling was Wear Ever pots and pans; that never turned out very well. Just when I had the apartment dwellers in the lobby in the palm of my hand, the wife came in and said, "Supper was ready." I went through a Rainbow vacuum cleaner demonstration, and the next day, I was going to be the one in the bubble. I never showed up.

After buying a 1959 Oldsmobile, the wife told all her friends that I paid three or four hundred dollars more than I actually paid for it. She was a foreigner that never understood the American way, how they liked to brag about how cheap they paid for something.

On the day that I was going to take my real estate license exam, I left Long Beach, California, and decided to go back in the navy for my second enlistment. We stopped in Casper to visit with Dad. He sat the wife on his lap. In front of me, he told her, "Mickey is overseas most of the time. Why don't you come back here and lived with me when he is gone?"

He didn't know that in Rapid City, I was going to file for a divorce.

I'm not sure what he had in mind, but knowing his history, I would have been hoodwinked. Arriving in Rapid City, South Dakota, I filed for a divorce. That day the papers were going to be given to the wife, I left Rapid City on a bus that went to Denver to be sworn in and be given a physical examination. At the physical examination, the man stood back about ten feet, and he told me to undress. Then he told me to turn around, bend over and spread your cheeks with your hands. I have often wondered about that physical exam. When he said, "Put your clothes on," I had a feeling that I passed.

After the navy was through with me, I went downtown in Denver for a few drinks. As I was walking down the sidewalk, a man came running out of a bar, and he was running sideways, yelling at the man running behind him, "Go ahead, shoot me."

The man shot him twice in the back, and his blood just missed my shoe. There was another bar, farther down the street that I went to.

On the way back to Rapid City, a girl on the bus, she was a keeper, kept looking at me. I got off the bus in Lusk, Wyoming, and decided to go on to Rapid City the next day. When my divorce was final, I knew that most of my money would be going for the support of the child. The next morning, I was in a hotel room, but my sailor hat was missing. I went down below to the café, and hanging on the coat rack was my hat. At the very least, I knew where I had spent part of the night.

In Rapid City, the wife and child went back to Long Beach, California, on a bus.

The navy sent me to the East Coast as I requested, to Philadelphia, Pennsylvania, to a receiving station to wait for my new assignment on the East Coast. When I was there, I went on the subway and found out what that was all about.

When my orders came in, they told me to go to San Diego, California. I had changed my mind about the East Coast. I was a happy camper and was sent to the US Comstock LSD 19 stationed out of San Diego, California, its home port.

Chapter 12

USS COMSTOCK
LSD 19

As I was walking up the pier to the ship, my seabag had everything that I owned in the world in it. A shipmate noticed it was getting the best of me, and he came down and carried it to my berthing compartment. It just so happened that he was in the same division as I was. I tried to pay him back with fewer midnight watches than he might have had. My rank that I made on the Carter Hall was E-5 or second class machinist's mate; that made me a boss.

They first assigned me to the port (left side) engine room. The first time that the ship was going someplace, I told the crew to sit down and relax, that I would light off all the machinery needed for the trip. They were impressed, but after all, the only difference in the ships were the *Comstock* had a turbine engine and the *Carter Hall* had a Skinner Uniflow reciprocating engine. The turbine engine was a lot less work to keep it running, and later, I was transferred to the main engine room or the starboard (right side) engine room.

One of the lower-ranking men and our boss, who was E-6 or first class machinist's mate, had a disagreement. He told him that when they got overseas, he was going to feed him to the fish. The boss believed him and went AWOL or away without leave. That left me in charge of the engine room. The navy never sent me to any school' I had achieved my increase in rank by studying the books that they gave me. Because I am seventy-four, my boss must be eighty-five to ninety years old, and perhaps it wouldn't get him in trouble because of his age or perhaps he is dead. Ben and I were walking from the ship to our favorite bar in National City one morning. My boss was going to work with a lunch pail. To say the least, we were surprised and asked him what he was doing. He told us he was going to work, and we told him that we wouldn't say anything. I never did until now.

Let's look at how this went down; about all I did on the first ship was wash, chip paint, or paint. Now I was in charge of the main engine room of a ship.

The only reason that I could ever see that I was assigned to be a machinist's mate was when they asked me what my hobbies were, I told them I liked to ride around in a car. Riding around in a car with enough beer to last the night and fixing a car, those were two different things. Now I was in charge of the maintenance of an engine room. It was the same with the cars; as long as they ran after I started them up, I was okay with it. The only thing that happened in the engine room that I might have had a problem fixing was an electric condensation pump. The chief fixed it during the time he was on watch while we were underway. We had a steam-driven pump on the line during the time the electric pump was being repaired.

All the other necessary maintenance, I managed to get done. One time in Hawaii, I worked on a pump all night to get it repaired for the trip the next day. We never had a spare pump for the job it performed. After I repaired it, I had the quarter deck watch from four to eight a.m., with no sleep at all. They asked me why I never said something, but that would have been normal. I had the diameter of the steel shaft that I had to work on, made temporary in the machine shop by Ben. I had the parts made for the pump before we tied up to the pier the day before. At the back gate of the San Diego Navy Station was National City, which had the closest bar. I noticed my same ship patch on one of the sailors in the bar, and I asked him if he wanted to play a game of pool. I ran the balls off the table, and that got his attention. The rest of the time I was on the ship, we did things together or separate; his name was Ben for Benjamin. The chief electrician who stood watches underway in the engine room said we were the Gold Dust Twins. I assume they were two cartoon characters before my time.

In Rapid City, I had about five hundred dollars in a bank account, and I asked Mom to send it to me as I wanted to buy a car. After buying the 1955 Lincoln, before they would give me a license plate, I had to have a smog control device put on. Ronald Reagan was governor of California, and there was a law passed that said every car sold had to have a smog control device. It wasn't driven very far, and the exhaust, instead of it going out the tailpipe, was staying in the motor. The motor was ruined in a very short time. It just barely made it to a used-car lot, and I traded it in for a 1959 Ford Thunderbird. It turned out it wasn't in much better shape than the Lincoln. It had been in a bad wreck that I never noticed until it was too late, and it was the last car that I ever bought from a used-car lot.

The ship patch on the arm was used to take the sailor back to his ship of they were lost. I found out the taxicab driver was the friendliest person in town, and it didn't matter what country they were in. One of the sailors in Japan unfriended one of them. He got in the cab, hit the

113

driver over the head with his sailor cap, and told him to "hi-ha-co," that is "hurry." The taxicab driver pulled him out of the cab, and he had to flag down another taxi.

The *Comstock* anchored out in the harbor of Okinawa. The sun was still up when Ben and I were in the first bar we came to. He said that he was going to another bar. It was like that: we usually left the ship together but hardly ever stayed together, even though the navy wanted a buddy system.

The girl that I was with gave me a drug of some kind of after Ben left, and the next thing I knew, I was at the back door with both of us pulling on my wallet. She evidently never wanted to do any work for the money. After I got my billfold out of her hands, I saw the shore patrol and crawled under an army truck. They saw me get under the truck, pulled me out, and took me back to the ship; the sun hadn't even gone down yet.

The division officer wouldn't believe me when I told him that a girl gave me a drug. He sent me over to a shrink on shore, and he asked me to subtract seven starting at one hundred to zero, in my head. When I convinced him that I couldn't do that, he sent me back to the ship, and I never heard anything more about it.

The ship was anchored out another time, and I was walking through the carpenter shop when the light went out. I knew that we only had one generator on the line, and it was directly below me, down a ladder. A ship without electricity is in trouble. One of the cruise ships in 2010 showed the world that. Descending down the ladder, I went over to the generator and opened the valve, putting raw steam to the turbine blades. I knew this procedure was only for emergencies only. By the sound of the turbine, I could tell it was up to speed, and I pointed to the electrician on duty to put the electrical power on the system. When he did that, I started up all the electric pumps that had to do with the generator. The chief came down the ladder, and the system was back normal.

There was never a word about the incident; to my knowledge, nothing was ever said. It was worth at least another bronze star. The chief was probably disappointed that he never got to do the emergency, but the longer you wait to put the raw steam in the turbine, the more danger there is of doing harm.

The ship had a diesel generator, but it never came on to my knowledge; it was up on a top deck.

On one of the trips to the Philippines, I had gone ashore around noon, and because the shore patrol wasn't around that early, I decided to go to a bar restricted for sailors. One of the girls and I got along well, and she took me to her house for a fee. When we got back to the bar, the music was playing, and we were out on the floor dancing. Five marines came through the front door; one of them came over and kicked me in the crotch. It doubled me up, and when I straightened up, I had both fists doubled up. I'm not sure what I was going to do with them. The Marines went back out the front door. They were lucky because I was madder than a wet hen that I saw on the farm. I told the girl that I didn't think it will ever work again
and if she would mind going back to the house for a trial run. It was the only time overseas that I never had to pay for it.

In the Philippines, we rode what we called a jeepney up and down the Main Street in Subic Bay. Where most of the bars were located, and you got on or off wherever suited you. I was out on the street and a guy driving a jeepney asked me if I wanted a girl. She was sitting alone on the backseat, so I got in, and he drove me out of town where I wasn't supposed to go, but I couldn't do anything about it. On a mattress on the floor, she was under me but managed to leave before anything happened. She told me that she had to do something. It never took me the rest of the night to figure out that she got my billfold. Putting on my clothes, I never knew where I was at and felt like I was in serious trouble the navy.

Going outside, the jeepney was parked; he drove me to the base where the ship was located. He handed me my billfold without any money in it, but I never argued with him. I was so thankful of getting back to the ship.

There was one sailor that went on liberty in the Philippines that was infected with syphilis, and he was restricted to the ship for six months or more. When the doctor told him he was cured and could go on liberty again, we were in the Philippines. It wasn't a good idea to turn him loose again in that country, and he was restricted again for another six months or more when he was infected with syphilis the second time.

One of my crew members had bought a mat made out of bamboo in Subic Bay; it was made to roll out on the floor to lay
down on. At the top of the engine room shaft, there was a little space where I rolled the mat out and laid down. The chief of our division came down the first short ladder and

116

saw the crew sanding around the pride of Wyoming and South Dakota.

The next time that I could have taken the test for first class machinist's mate, he wouldn't let me because he said I was sleeping on the mat during working hours.

The same chief was making his rounds of the ship to check it out, and he had the quarterdeck watch; that is where people come and go on or off the ship. Near the machine shop, where Ben worked, Ben and I were drinking out of a water glass. He said, "Let me smell that," and after he got his smell he walked over and poured both glasses over the side of the ship.

Our favorite spot was the portside gun mount. It wasn't beneath us to take whiskey, water, and bitters back there. I never brought whiskey aboard the ship; Ben did that, so it was all his fault. One time, in the middle of the ocean, he passed out in the berthing compartment.

A sailor bought a beautiful red ruby in Hong Kong, and he was showing it to the shipmates when one of them dropped it and it shattered all over the floor.

Ben and I rented a one bedroom apartment in San Diego. There was a couch in the living room and a bed in the back bedroom. The one that arrived at the apartment first got the couch. That was in case the other had a girl with him when they got home. It was reversed if there was a girl that was brought home first.

I had met a girl at the dance hall in National City, and I took the bus back and forth from her house a few times. One of her friends, she told me, build her house making love. She received money from the navy or marine recruits from boot camp, and when she needed a plumber, electrician, carpenter, Sheetrocker, etc., she would pay them off one way or the other. A few of them, she even paid money to; who said there was only one way to skin a cat or built a house?

We made a short trip overseas, and at the time, I was going with a girl from Guam. I had shore patrol the one night we got liberty. When I got back to San Diego, she infected me with gonorrhea, finding that out after going home on leave. I went to the air force base in Rapid City to get a shot, and for some reason, I almost passed out, which I have been known to do a few times.

Paul had a babysitter that I went with while I was on a thirty-day leave, but she had a square jaw that Mom never liked, so all I got out of her was a ride to the airport. I went back to my comfort food, the bottle. I had stopped off on the way to Rapid City to see Dad in Casper, Wyoming, and a police officer was there. Dad was in the back of the trailer in his bed. The officer told me he was going to take the license plates off the truck because he wouldn't stop driving it. His driver's license was suspended at that time. He never did know that I came to his house for a visit; I went on to Rapid City.

Ben and I bought several bottles of booze overseas because it was cheaper. I took a quart of 100-proof whiskey with me to see Dad in Cuba City, Wisconsin. At the time, he was building the upper floor on my sister and Merlyn's basement. For years, they lived in a basement, raising five children. He drank so much of the whiskey; I stayed partially sober. I never anyone that I thought could drink as much whiskey straight from a bottle as Dad. When we were going somewhere in his truck, he ran through at least two red lights, I'm not sure how he missed getting killed in a car accident and taking someone else with him.

The baby that I put the eye out of when I was three or four years old happened to call Dad, and he told him that I was there. He said that he was coming to see me. I left on the next plane to San Diego, California, and back to the apartment.

One if the girls was married when I first met her, and shortly afterward, her husband was burnt up on the couch. The police said it was a cigarette that cased the discomfort. I went on a date with her and was at her house on the morning. After I got dressed, she wouldn't let me leave. I practically had to fight my way out of the house. From then on, Ben and I wouldn't let her come inside our apartment. I told Ben that she was crazy, and he believed me.

The ship went to Long Beach for a major ship repair, and that was where my ex-wife lived. She let me move in with her for a while. One day, Ben showed up with a girl to use the bed. When the left, the sheets were gray. I told Ben his tool was going to rot off. We rented another apartment in Long Beach, and my ex caught me with another girl, and she tried to stab me with a knife. My new girl left, and I never saw her again.

In the military, it was against the rules to loan money to other personnel, but half of my money was going to my wife for child support. The three things that I couldn't be short of was booze, cigarettes, and women, and all three required money. It behooved me to loan money with a

119

certain percentage attached to the transaction. There was a sailor that I noticed never went to town and I borrowed money form a savings and loan to give him to loan out. I received half of the profits.

One day, I came back from a thirty-day leave, and several sailors called me lucky. After a few of those, I asked a sailor why they were calling e lucky. He told me that while I was on leave, several of the people that loaned money were written up for the offense. What that meant was they had to go talk to the captain; it was called a captain's mast. I was about to get out of the navy, so I quit loaning money.

Ben and I, almost every time we had a chance to go on liberty, got a person to stand our duties while we went to town. Christmas passed, and we were in Japan. I found Ben and said, "Ben, are we going to get a standby for New Year's Eve?"

He said, "Ah, Mutton, every day is New Year's Eve.

That was when the title of this book was born. He called me Mutton often; I'm not sure where it came from.

One of the girls at my favorite bar was the kind of a girl that you would introduce to your mother. One night, she took me to her house after the dance. The next morning, she said that she gave "it" to her newspaper boy. I said "You mean for Christmas?"

She said, "During the week if he wants it."

That was the story of my life.

The ship anchored off the coast of Guam, and my brother was stationed there, but I never knew how to contact him. We only stayed one night. He was in the Vietnam War but stationed in Guam. The B-52s were flying form there and bombing the shorts off the enemy. The Navy took a battleship out of retirement with sixteen-inch guns and blew some more shorts off. Every time they fired the big gun, I was told it cost the price of a new car. One of the enemy was captured and brought to our ship. All he had on was a t-shirt, shorts, with no shoes.

Before Paul had left to go to Guam, my dad's brother Leroy helped Paul disassemble some buildings on the Rapid City Air Force Base. The contract was bid in my dad's name because they never wanted their air force men to get hurt. Paul fell and shattered his arm but managed to stay in the air force because he only had about two years left before he could retire; he was a supervisor. One day, Leroy drove a truck to Mom's house where the lumber was stacked and stored. Mom told him if he didn't leave, she was going to call the police. Leroy never did get one stick of the lumber or wages helping Paul tear down the buildings.

I'm not sure when Leroy jumped the fence, but when I knew him, he was married with three children. He was driving home from church, went to sleep, and was killed. His boyfriend told Dad after the funeral that he could come over and get Leroy's things, but Dad said, "You can have it." Leroy played a guitar all his life, and I'm not sure how much it would have been worth; some of them are worth a lot of money today.

When Paul retired from the air force, he went to college and received a doctorate degree in philosophy and general education and taught in a college until he retired permanently in Tacoma, Washington.

Each payday, I had the navy take out a $100 bond from my paycheck. That was $200 each month. At the end of the second enlistment, I had over $5,000 in savings.

About a year before I was to be discharged from the navy, I came home from the bar at one a.m. and thought about how soon I would be discharged from the navy. I would be on my own, when I was three or four. The religious experience, until I was nine years old, never helped; at the time, it never impressed me. In Mom's eye, I was the black sheep of the family. Drinking, smoking, and sex from the bars, from the tenth grade of high school, put me in that position. A year after high school graduation, going through the windshield of a car after drinking with a friend, in a head-on collision with another car in Casper, Wyoming. The left scars on my face that matched those from my knees to my waist.

That night, I was turned down from dancing with the girls. I was probably too drunk, and I always tried to avoid any lasting relationship with girl on what little money I received. A lot of money was going to the child on the divorce. As a matter of fact, I felt sorry for any girl that liked me.

I never felt adequate doing the job that I was responsible for an the ship, but for almost four years, I was on charge of the maintenance and personnel of the starboard engine room. If I made another rank in the navy as chief, which was recommended for, I could be solely in charge of the repairs on small a small ship, and I never felt like I was qualified for that.

Going drunk to the apartment that Ben and I shared at one a.m., I blew out the pilot light in the oven and top burners of the cookstove. Each burners I turned on as high as they would go and went to bed. When the apartment became full of gas, I knew that it would explode from the pilot light on the water heater, which was located just above the floor. Natural gas goes up, so I knew it would take a little while to explode, not realizing it at the time that it would probably kill me and the lady that lived in the duplex next door.

Ben came home from the bar sometime after I went to be and smelled the natural gas. He turned off the burners, opened the outside doors, and shook me to see if I was still alive. I would have to live another day, and we never talked between us about what I did.

With a total of eight years in the US Navy, I received two honorable discharges, three Bronze Stars, Expedition Medal, Vietnam Service Medal with Device, and two Good Conduct Discharge Medals. I entered the navy in 1959 and was discharged December 8, 1967, in Long Beach, California.

Walking out the front gate, I got on a city bus with almost everything I owned in a seabag and rented a one-bedroom studio apartment with a bath and a bed.

Chapter 13

BANKRUPT BUSINESSMAN

All my meals were eaten in restaurants, cafes, or a catering truck that came to the factory when I eventually worked. My 1959 Ford Thunderbird was in San Diego and I went after that. The girl in San Diego, I never told her that I was going to get out of the navy. When I arrived and never came home all night. A girl form the bar kept me warm. The next morning, I left her a note that had been there, with no forwarding address, and drove to Long Beach, California.

In a Long Beach newspaper, I read an ad selling a business of a five-bay coin car wash, fish market, one-man garage, and a restaurant. The buildings were all I was buying; the land belonged to someone else that I had to send $300 a month lease payments to. The restaurant had the largest monthly rent, and unaware of it, the proprietors bought a bar-restaurant about four blocks down the street. They milked my restaurant out of every dime they could by not paying their monthly rent or just enough to leave me dangling.

To supplement my income, I saw an advertisement in the newspaper for a man to work in a factory in Los Angeles. It consisted of putting together parts to make drill presses, so I became a machinery assembler in a Burgmaster factory. It was to save Cal-Vision Enterprises Inc. from bankruptcy. Almost all my money, except beer and cigarettes, went into the business.

After writing Dad that I had bought a business, one day, we had missed each other at the car wash, and he knocked on the apartment door. When I got off work at the factory, I went by the car wash and emptied the cash boxes into a sack. As usual, he never told me he was coming, and the first thing that he told me was that he sat out in front of the car wash, and not one person drove in to wash their cars. I emptied the day's receipts on the bed, and he said, "You're lying."

That evening, we played a few games of pool, had a few beers, and he wanted to go to a topless bar. The next morning, Dad went back to Wyoming.

The first mistake that I made was that I added too much soap to the system, and it impeded the hoses. The other mistake I made was when I got the car wash, it had five reciprocating pumps instead of centrifugal pumps. The clogged hoses put too much pressure on the pumps and that caused extra maintenance.

The hot-water tank quit working; in the process of lighting the pilot, the flame shot out about two feet and burned the skin off my left hand to the wrist. At the factory, I wore a brown jersey glove and never went to see the doctor. I went to the house of my latest girlfriend, but because she wasn't home, I lay out on her lawn and suffered. When she finally came home, I accused her of fooling around and went back to the car wash. If you can remember tight lips in Seattle, she was just the opposite, and she liked to put ice in her vagina. The flood was all I had to contend with.

The first night that I met her, we went to a motel and we couldn't find the manager to rent us the motel room. She started walking down the corridor, and one of the doors was open and we went in there. The sheets were a little soiled from the night before, but she didn't seem to mind. When we were discovered, I told the manager I would come down and pay her later. She charged me the regular price of the room, and I thought I should have gotten a discount.

The proprietors in the restaurant did me a favor and moved out. If there is anything that I learned in the situation that was in, it was without any money, you've vulnerable to every whim of human nature. I told the proprietor of the fish market that I would raise his rent if I thought it would do any good.

The thing that came to mind for the restaurant was to make it into a coin laundry, but without any money, that idea never lasted long.

During this time, it must have felt the same with me as it did during World War II; a lot of people, especially in the churches, thought for sure the end-time was near. There were a lot of people out of work because of the Dust Bowl, farmers who couldn't make a living and moving to other parts of the country from the south, etc. in the Bible, there are a lot written about what is going to happen at the end-time.

In 1967 and '68, there was a lot going on because of the Vietnam War, and I had spent a lot of time in church as a child. I could remember things that I was told that were in the Bible, and it appeared to me as going on in different part of the country. The rioting in the streets, burning up of entire neighborhoods, free love, hippies, flower children, college kids being killed on some of the campuses, and communal living, etc.

It started to get me thinking, *Is this religious stuff real?* That was the question that I was asking myself.

This same period, someone picked a song out in the bar on the jukebox that had the words, "If I never get to heaven, it will be because of you, etc." It added fuel to my inner fire.

The life that I was living was getting old; with the drinking, hangovers every morning, raw nicotine coming up into my throat, and two of my fingers a dark color that held the lit cigarette that was seldom put out. My relationships couldn't have been any worse. Mostly without an education and money, I never did try to find a lasting one. It would take away from the decadence that I was used to.

The restaurant was empty, and without any money to speak of, I went to the same real estate broker that sold me the property to ask him if they could find someone to lease the restaurant. Near the waiting area, the secretary was close by, and she asked me, "Has God been good to you?"

That took me by surprise I said, "I went to church when I was a child,"

And she asked me, "What were some of the songs that you song?"

After telling her a few, I could see afterward, it was another way of asking me what denomination I belonged to. She gave me the address of the church that she attended.

After talking to the broker to find me a lesser for the restaurant, I went on with my life. It bothered me what the secretary asked me. It seemed like my life had been a shambles from almost the day that I was born. I always felt like Dad and Mom hated me, and now on the verge of bankruptcy, living in one room, with a dilapidated car, it never looked good. A job that never paid much wasn't any help, and if ever had any friends, I left them behind. A year earlier, I had gotten out of the navy and watched those friends sail away.

Chapter 14

RELIGION

In the King James Bible of 1611, it says, "Except the Father which hath sent me draw him: (you or me and unless this is done) no man can come to me." We have free will, but if the circumstances in your life are not going well, didn't God put the problems there in the first place? The book of life and Lamb's book of life could be the same book, and in one verse, it says your name was in the book from the foundation of the world. This hints that those destined to be saved were written in the book or Revelation 20:15, "And whosoever was not found written in the book of life was cast into the lake of fire." It could be only those people that become saved is written in the book of life. Another verse hints that everybody's name is in the book, and it says, "And I will not blot out his name out of the book of life, but I will confess his name out of the book of life, but I will confess his name before my Father, and before his angels. "Who said the Bible is easy to understand? My life at the time wasn't going well, so let's say God decided for me that each Sunday night, I would attend the evening service in a Protestant church. Dad was an ordained Assembly of God minister when I was a child, so I knew what the procedures were that the churches followed.

At first, I went to the church that the secretary gave me the address of, and after a couple of Sunday nights there, I decided to go someplace else. As a child, at times, I felt the convince spirit of my sins or a repentant heart but never did act on it. The wrath of God was the preacher, it seemed to me. Everybody assumed the preacher's kid was saved, and according to most doctrines, they were. Several churches gave me every opportunity to become a Christian, according to their standards or doctrine, but I was holding out to feel the convictive spirit. When the church services were over. I went to my favorite dance hall and bar over two months.

There was a so-called revival at a Nazarene church. I was sitting by a woman, and when the preacher asked, "If anyone needed to be prayed for, raise your hand."

I raised my hand, and he then asked for those that raised their hands to come forward. I had heard that line before, and because I never felt anything, I went out the door. The woman next to me couldn't understand why I went out of the door and never went down to the front of the church to become a Christian. There was no doubt in my mind that I was sinner that needed a savior.

One of my pumps at the car wash needed a part, and on the way to get the part, I went past a Protestant church. I decided that the next Sunday night, I would attend that church.

On Saturday night, I went to my favorite bar, and around ten p.m., I went next door to a bar and dance hall. One of the girls fell in love with me, and she lived in a house close to the bar. Before leaving the next morning, I told her I'd be back to see her Sunday night, around ten p.m.

With my usual cigarette package in my front pocket and wearing a suit, I sat on the back seat of the church Sunday evening. The pastor asked everyone to stand up to sing a

song, "smile a while, and give your face a rest, raise your hands to the
one you love the best, turn around, and shake a hand and, smile, smile, smile."

An elderly lady came over and asked me, "Do you love Jesus?"

"No." I knew that if I said yes, she would assume that I was saved.

When the sermon was over, the preacher asked those that needed salvation to come forward, and I felt the spirit that I had been waiting for. As I was kneeling at the altar, I asked God to help me. In a few minutes, I got up, and several of the church members were calling me brother. I couldn't believe that I never felt something. Going over to the elderly lady, I said, "Don't worry, I'll make it."

If you think about it, I did everything that I had seen done over the years, not only from my dad, but other preacher of going forward etc. with God's power of making the universe, when a person gets saved, don't they feel something? I couldn't believe it. Even Luke said in 11:20, "But if I with the finger of God cast out devils, no doubt the kingdom of God is come upon you."

When leaving the church, it occurred to me that I must be okay as almost everyone in the congregation was calling me brother.

The car wash was not far away, so I went there to get some quarters out of the coin boxes to call my mother. A gas station was a telephone on an outside wall. When Mom answered, I told her that I went to the altar tonight, and she said, "Pray for your dad and me."

At that instant, I believed in my heart that now I could pray and heal her; she had rheumatoid arthritis. You will note, that was one of the works that Jesus did, was healing people. St. John 10:37-38 and 14:11 are three verses that has the mystery to enter the kingdom of God for salvation.

"If I do not the works of my Father, believe me not. But if I do, though ye believe not me, believe the works: that ye may know and believe, that the Father is in me, and I in him." (John 10:37-38)

"Believe me that I am in the Father, and the Father in me: or else believe me for the very works' sake." (John 14:11)

When I said I will, there was something that hit me in my back, and it knocked my right foot forward a half step. I saw something leave my body to the right, and my arms went up, bent at the elbows, about even with my neck, with my left hand still holding on to the telephone. According to the Bible, what left my body was the heart that I was born with because that is where the sin of Adam is located, plus the sin that you accumulate here on this earth. My shoulders caved in toward the middle of my body. My neck was stiff, but I managed to peer toward my left side, and a stream of light was entering my back. It traveled in a semicircular path. The middle of my body began to expand and my shoulders were going back to their normal position. Mom said a few niceties, and I believe all I said was "Okay" and hung up the telephone.

Walking toward the car wash in a daze, with both arms out away from my body, it was hard for me to believe what had just happened. Was this the first death that the Bible mentions, and it says that: "He that overcometh shall not be hurt of the second death" (Revelation 2:11 and 20:6)

The next morning at work, I told a Baptist friend, who worked with me that Sunday night, I was saved, and previously when I went to his church, a man was snoring so loud I couldn't hear the sermon.

At coffee break, ,the catering truck showed up, and I found out then that I was on a period of fasting for the next three days and nights. After leaving the jobsite, I stopped the car and threw the package of cigarettes in the gutter that had been in my shirt pockets all day. The girl that I went with Saturday night, I went to her house and told her "I won't be seeing you anymore."

That night, I went inside a bar not far from my studio apartment and walked out. It had been years since I could do that, and the next morning, I never had a hangover nor did I light up a cigarette.

The next Wednesday night, I went back to the same church, and when they asked for testimonials, I stood up and said, "I never got saved at the altar last Sunday night but was saved at a gasoline service station."

When the service was over, no one asked me what I meant. They never understood what I had said, and the churches haven't a clue of how complicated salvation is according to the Bible. "Of being born again and receiving the Spirit or Holy Ghost." Without both of these, "he cannot enter into the kingdom of God" (St. John 3:5).

I started listening to the radio, the Christian broadcasts, and determined that there was something terribly wrong. The preacher on radio and TV were telling people, "Just repeat after me the sinner's prayer, if you want to be saved," but salvation is physical as it happened to me. Is one of us wrong?

There was a period of thirty days that my body was being cleaned up. It seemed like the very pores of my skin were filthy; why not, I had been drinking and smoking for years. That was what the fasting was all about, cleaning up my body. The idols that I lived by left me that Sunday night about nine p.m.: no drinking, smoking, swearing, and sex for at least fifteen years.

From this tie forward, it was like God himself took over my life. The first thing that happened, I went back to the real estate broker and told him not to find a leaser but put the business up for sale. In two weeks, I received from Mom for Christmas, a King James Encyclopedic Reference Bible of 1611 and Dad gave me a Cruden's Complete Concordance of that Bible. I never had a Bible, except the little one that the navy gave me, which I never read in the room at that time.

I started reading the Bible, I believe in Genesis; after all, isn't that the beginning of the book? Doesn't a person start reading a book at the beginning? What about the Word that Jesus spoke for this dispensation? It wasn't very long, afterward and I was reading the Gospels. That Sunday night that I was saved was December 1, 1968, at nine p.m.

and I previously mentioned the thirty-day period, at the end of it was December 30, 1968. The day before was Sunday, which was the twenty-ninth. My son was living with his mother, and we went to a new Protestant church which I had not attended before.

At the beginning of the service, the preacher asked everyone to stand up to sing a song. I had a songbook opened up at the page in my hand, and there was a force that knocked it to the floor. It also made me walk toward the front of the church with both arms raised. When I got to the front of the church, the preacher and a deacon had their fingers digging in my sides. When I came to conscious state, my sides were hurting, and went back to my seat. There was a possibility that I might have received the Holy Ghost that morning, but it wasn't on the program. We went back for the evening service, and when I was leaving, the preacher asked me how I felt. I answered him, "At peace with myself."

The next morning, going to work in Los Angeles, California, a vision came into my mind of a man that had left one of the churches to enter the ministry. I said, "God help that boy."

On the word "boy," a white thing, like a dove, came through the windshield. It went in my mouth and down my throat. The reason that I used the word "dove" is that's in the Bible, when Jesus was baptized in water, by John the Baptist. When baptizing someone in water fully submerged, the first breath comes from opening the mouth. That's when the Holy Ghost "entered the mouth of Jesus." It never related to the other spirit but separate, it is only for those that become saved.

135

It happened so fast; that is the reason they got it wrong in St. Matthew 3:16.

The same day that I received the Holy Ghost, I had my closing on the business. The broker had put an advertisement in the Los Angeles newspaper, and the buyers wanted the corporation more than the business. The buyer gave me a ride to my house, as at the time I never had a car.

After reading an advertisement in the newspaper of a Cadillac that was for sale, I went to possibly but it, and the 1959 Ford quit running about a block from his house. The Cadillac never impressed me, so I asked him if he would like to have my car parked about a block away. I told him if he drove me home, I'll give the title. He said okay. I informed him that there wasn't anything that worked on the car: engine, transmission, heater, radio, etc.

To get work, a few days, I rented a car and then went to a Volkswagen dealer to buy my first new car, a 1969 VW. I put less than two thousand miles on it, and I was lying on the couch. In front of the house, a man hit my car in the back, and it was pushed into a Ford Mustang. My insurance company bought me another VM, and they had to fix or replace the Mustang.

Two days later, there was a knock on the door, and the man said he would like to see the paperwork of the wreck. He said, "That's not my son's name."

He had given the police a phony name, and he had no insurance or valid registration for his car. After calling the police station, I gave them the man's real name, and I don't know what happened after that, but the wreck came to haunt me later.

After I received the Holy Ghost, I started reading the Gospels (the good news); that was what the Son of God told us to study and read. When reading a verse, the very same thing happened to me physically, then how can I not believe it when it's in the Bible? Luke has a lot of flaws, so I quit reading it. I believe he spent too much time with Paul. Paul was the Devil's advocate and not sent from God. St. John 5:43 verifies that statement: "I am come in my Father's name, and ye (receive) me not: (Jesus) if another shall come in his own name, him ye will receive" (Paul). In the dictionary, receive means (1) to take into one's possession (something given, sent, etc.) get; (2) to encounter: experience; (3) to bear; take the effect or force of. The second receive doesn't mean the same thing as the first because Satan's can't physically give anybody anything.

It says in St. Matthew that Jesus fasted forty days and forty nights. I only fasted three days and nights. It doesn't say how long He was in the wilderness. I had a similar experience, but it lasted two years. In those two years, I was tempted by Satan, and the Holy Ghost was teaching me the statues or the commandments of God. At the end of time that Jesus spent in the wilderness, it says, "Then the devil leaveth him, and, behold, angels came and ministered unto him." (St. Matthew 4:11)

In San Pedro, California, shortly after I received the Holy Ghost, I asked my ex-wife if I could move the child over to an apartment that I rented and take care of him. She said

137

okay and told me she was going to go to Japan as a missionary. I'm not sure when she got religious.

After going to a church in San Pedro near the house, one Sunday morning in Sunday school, we had a woman teacher. She was teaching the verses in St. John 2: about changing the water into wine. All I learned was how to bake bread. At the end of the class, I looked up toward the ceiling and saw what I believed was an angel. It wore a white robe with no head, feet or hands. I blurted out in the class, "Judgement day was coming." We were dismissed. It disappeared when the guy next to me started to look up.

That evening, instead of going to church, I stayed home and was studying the Bible. At midnight, I started walking to the kitchen for a glass of water. There was an audible voice that said, "Change the water into wine." Filling the glass to the brim, I went back in the front room and set the glass down on the coffee table. Raising both arms above my head, I said, "Father in heaven, change the water in wine, in Jesus name, amen."

There was nothing that happened in the glass, but there was a sensation from the tips of my finger to my toes. I felt smaller and went to the mirror in the bathroom to see if I was the same height. At the end of the time, when Jesus was in the wilderness, it read than an angel came and ministered unto him as it did me, and that night was a follow-up of what happened in the Sunday school class that morning. St. Matthew 4:11 can be read above.

I haven't mentioned very many verses in the Bible, but the best verses that explain what it meant to be born again and receive His Spirit or Holy Ghost is found in Ezekiel. The reason that Ezekiel never got the message nor verses in correct order was he never understood what he was writing down, nor did he experience it physically as I did.

There's similar chapters and verses found in other Old Testament books. The Holy Ghost wasn't to be in his day, and it is not related to the other spirit. The Spirit (Holy Ghost) most often is always capitalized.

You can compare what happened to me with these verses in Ezekiel 36:26-25-27, "Anew heart also will I give you. (the heart that I was born with was removed) Then will I sprinkle clean water upon you, (born again) and ye shall be clean from all your filthiness and from all you idols, will I cleanse you and a new Spirit will I put within you: (Holy Ghost was given to me thirty days later) and I will take away the stony heart out of your flesh, (born with) and I will give you a heart of flesh. (from God) And I will put my Spirit (Holy Ghost) within you, and cause you to walk in my statutes, and ye shall keep my judgments, and do them (two years above)."

One of the Sunday school teachers came up with this one when I was a child. It's not in the Bible. She said, "A person should live their life to not come under the judgment of man." In other words, obey the laws of God and man's laws.

Words are interesting. I looked up several in the Webster's New World Dictionary. Those that put it together would never think that what they wrote down was not necessarily the truth. Don't we have to go by what is written in the King James Bible of 1611? Is there some other truth someplace else that we can go by? But even that Bible

139

is not totally nonfiction, error free, and some of it is downright misleading; so as they say, buyer beware.

Some of the words that I looked up were: Mystery: In theology, any assumed truth that cannot be comprehended by the human mind. (Is that true?)

Theology: The study of God and of religious doctrines, etc.

The problem is found in a verse in the Bible: "Because it is given unto you to know the mysteries of the kingdom of heaven, but to them it is not given" (St. Matthew 13: 11).

It reads that when it is a mystery, it can't be comprehended by the majority of people, but a few will understand what Jesus told us or understand the parables.

In St. Mark, it is similar, but it is elaborated on a little more: "Unto you it is given to know the mystery of the kingdom of God: but unto them that are without, (on the outside) all these things are done in parables."

Allegory: When things have another meaning. "That seeing they may see and not perceive; and hearing they may hear, and not understand; (but) lest at any time they should be converted, (to change; transform) and their sins should be forgiven them." These are the few that will "comprehend the mystery" (4: 11–12).

I am one of the few, but the majority don't have a clue. They are the ones that are in charge of what is printed, read, and spoken. The odds of getting this book in the public domain, it would be easier throwing the horse over the barn.

What are the ten most common myths or mythology (the study of myths (any fictitious story))? The mysteries in theology that cannot be comprehended.

Do we go by all of the King James version of the Bible of 1611? No. What about Satan? Is he powerless? Doesn't he have a part in the outcome of the end-time or judgment day? Luke said that we are to go by all the Bible; St. Matthew said we are only to go by what came out of the mouth of God (Jesus). Luke traveled a lot with Paul, who wrote half of the New Testament, so why shouldn't he say that? St. Matthew 4: 4 and Luke 4: 4 says, "Man shall not live by bread alone, but by every word that proceedeth out of the mouth of God" (Jesus). Luke said, "That man shall not live by bread alone, but by every word of God." That would mean the entire Bible including the Acts through Jude, and there is a difference.

"For thou hast said in thine heart, I (Lucifer) will ascend into heaven, (God's domain) I will exalt my throne above the stars of God: (religious organizations) I will sit also upon the mount (all) of the congregation (churches) in the sides of the north: I will ascend above the heights of the clouds; I will be like the Most High" (Isaiah 14: 13–14). Lucifer said that he would be like God, so Paul was the advocate for Satan. "I am come in my Father's name, and ye receive me not: (Jesus) if another shall come in his own name, him ye will receive" (Paul) (St. John 5: 43). "Receive" is an interesting word, to take into one's possession (something given, sent), to encounter, experience. God had to use the word in both parts of the sentence; it is part of the mystery of God.

In Revelation 20: 10, who would the false prophet be other than Paul? "And the devil that deceived them was cast into the lake of fire and brimstone, where the beast (Antichrist) and the false prophet are, and shall be tormented day and night forever and ever."

Trinity or quadruple? Did God die on the cross, or was it the Son of God whose name is Jesus? The majority of people will tell you God died on the cross. Why is it blasphemy to speak against the Holy Ghost, but it is okay to swear using God's name or His Son Jesus's name? The majority believes that the Holy Ghost is God also, but in these verses, it doesn't make any common sense. St. Matthew 12: 31–32 says, "Wherefore I say unto you, All manner of sin and blasphemy shall be forgiven unto men: but the blasphemy against the Holy Ghost shall not be forgiven unto men. And whosoever speaketh a word against the Son of man, it shall be forgiven him: but whosoever speaketh against the Holy Ghost, it shall not be forgiven him, neither in this world, neither in the world to come." We find the spirit in Genesis 1: 2, 26. Jesus is Mary's Son that was going to present the Word and give it to mankind, etc. The Word I believe was with God before creation. The Holy Ghost is the better half of the salvation plan; in other words, "it is the only game in town." To receive it is the only way to enter into the kingdom of God, but first, your body must be clean. God created these three, so with God as the Father, the Godhead is Quadruple.

The Holy Ghost has nothing to do with speaking in tongues. It is received as Jesus received it when He was

142

baptized by John. I received it but without the water baptism. It went in my mouth and down my throat when God put a vision on me to open my mouth. St. Matthew 3: 16 and 20: 23 says, "And Jesus, when he was baptized went up straightway out of the water: and, lo, the heavens were opened unto him, and he saw the Spirit of God (Holy Ghost) descending like a dove, and lighting upon him: And he saith unto them, Ye shall drink indeed of my cup, and be baptized with the baptism that I am baptized with: I am the way the truth and the life." What if we said, "I (Jesus) am the way; I (Jesus) am the truth; I am the life"? Where does that leave the other religious organizations with a different Bible, etc., if Jesus is the, way? His Word is the only truth. The salvation plan brings "life or understanding," and people don't know they are dead to the truth. St. Matthew 13: 10 says, "And the disciples came, and said unto him, Why speakest thou unto them in parables? He answered and said unto them, Because it is given unto you to know the mysteries of the kingdom of heaven, but to them it is not given."

Sacrament and water baptism? People should shy away from anything that man says is a requirement that they do to each other physically because it doesn't come from God. John the Baptist warned us in three Gospels that water baptism has nothing to do with salvation. "I indeed baptize you with water unto repentance: but he that cometh after me is mightier than I, whose shoes I am not worthy to bear: (stoop down and unloose) he shall baptize you with the Holy Ghost, and with fire" (St. Matthew 3: 11). "John answered and said, A man can receive nothing, except it be given him from heaven" (St. John 3: 27).

143

Is the sacrament any different? "But I (Jesus) say unto you, I will not drink henceforth of this fruit of the vine, until that day when I drink it new with you in my Father's kingdom" (St. Matthew 26: 29). When the saints are taken out of this earth at the end-time, that is when there will be a time of feasting in the Father's kingdom; that is what He is referring to.

St. John 6: 48–58 has nothing to do with the sacrament. Those verses are all about being born again and receiving the Spirit or Holy Ghost: "This is the bread which cometh down from heaven, that a man eat thereof, and not die. Verily, verily, I say unto you, Except ye eat the flesh of the Son of man, (born again or new heart (Ezekiel 36: 26-25-27)) and drink his blood (new Spirit (Ezekiel 36: 26 and 27)) ye have no life in you. For my flesh is meat indeed, and my blood (Holy Ghost) is drink indeed."

Believe. That is true, but it has conditions: You must believe in your heart, and that is a lot different than believing with your mind. There are only four verses in the Bible that has the mystery or keys to enter the kingdom of heaven: "If I do not the works of my Father, believe me not. But if I do, though ye believe not me, believe the works: that ye may know and believe, that the Father is in me, and I in him... The words that I speak unto you I speak not of myself: but the Father that dwelleth in me (Holy Ghost) he doeth the works. Believe me that I am in the Father, and the Father in me: or else believe me for the very works sake" (St. John 10: 37–38; 14: 10–11).

Jesus received (God's creation) the Holy Ghost when He was baptized by John (Matthew 3: 16), that is why it reads, "The Father dwelleth in me." In St. John 14: 10, it says,

"Believeth thou not that I am in the Father, and the Father in me? The words that I speak unto you I speak not of myself: but the Father that dwelleth in me (he, Holy Ghost) doeth the works. How could the Father dwelleth in Him some other way?"

I believed in one of the works that Jesus did of healing, and it triggered the spirit into action, and this spirit is not related to the Special Spirit (Holy Ghost) that is only given to those that are born again first and converted or transformed.

"Feed the poor," that is what it says, but I wouldn't risk my soul on it. There must be a lot of money made using the poor people as an excuse to send money or goods in, with some selling the items. You are not fooling God any. "Jesus answered them and said, Verily, verily, I say unto you, Ye seek me, not because ye saw the miracles, but because ye did eat of the loaves, and were filled" (St. John 6: 26).

How many are making a good living feeding the poor? I'm sorry, but without salvation, it is in vain. It says to "seek ye first the kingdom of God, and his righteousness"; after that, feed the poor if that is what God wants. The Kingdom of God is, you must be born again and receive the Spirit or Holy Ghost first. St. Matthew 6: 33 and St. John 3: 3–5 or Ezekiel 36: 26–25–27 and St. Matthew 6: 33 says, "But seek ye first the kingdom of god, and his righteousness: and all these things shall be added unto you."

Age of Accountability

It sounds reasonable if a child would die, they would go to live in the kingdom of God or heaven before the age of accountability. If it was only true. There is one verse that doesn't agree with that assessment. "The wicked are estranged (to cause a transference of affection from the mother) from the womb: they go astray as soon as they be born, (lucky to be born) speaking lies" (Psalm 58:3). If this verse means what it says, it doesn't agree with the age of accountability as you hear in most churches, so I believe it is another doctrine that is made up by man. You must be born again and receive the Spirit. It not, they can't enter into the kingdom of God, no matter what age a person is.

Grace and Faith

I'm aware that Paul said you need both terms to be saved, but in the Gospels, I know of no verse that suggests that. When I found out salvation is physical, it doesn't make any common sense or scriptural, in the Gospels, grace is seldom mentioned, faith a little more often, but faith must be connected to "believing in your heart," as I mentioned before. Churches that put a lot of merit in either one, I wouldn't want to be in their shoes. Both words are used a lot as part of their denominational names.

Who is in charge of the denominations? Do you really think God could be in control of all the confusion we find on the earth in the religious communities? God is the master of order in all that He created. There is no way that we should have as many churches as we do and different religious throughout the world. Most all the denominations will tell you their doctrine is the one you should follow. "I am the door: by me if any man enter in, he shall be saved, and shall go in and out and find pasture." (St. John 10:9). He is saying that God will save you, but you will have to be one of the chosen seeking to be saved, and admitting that you

146

are a sinner that needs salvation. He never came to save the righteous but sinners, so Satan is in control of the religious community (Isaiah 14:13-14). Luke, who traveled too much with Paul, is the only Gospel that I find that much fault with. The first chapter especially has verses in it that none of the other three Gospels compares with what Luke tells us. He assumes most everybody has the Holy Ghost, but it wasn't to be until after Jesus went to be with his Father in heaven (St. John 16:7). The preacher believe when you raise your hand to be saved, that is when the Spirit joins your body for eternity. But the Spirit is only for those that become truly saved.

St. John 16:7 says, "Nevertheless I tell you the truth; it is expedient for you that I go away: for if I go not away, the Comforter (Holy Ghost) will not come unto you; but if I depart, I will send him send him unto you." In the Gospel of St. Matthew, it explains the first on to receive it (Spirit) which was Jesus in chapter 3:16. Did Jesus prophesy at the time? No, He went in the wilderness to learn what God wanted to Him to say and do through the teaching of the Holy Ghost. He was also tempted by Satan, who gave Jesus an opportunity to join him.

Jesus was born without sin, so He never needed to be born again as we do.

The Holy Ghost can't reveal anything outside of what is already in the Word that is true. The biggest problem that Luke has is people can't receive the Holy Ghost without being born again first because it can't come into a person until their body is clean (Ezekiel 36:25 above). They say Luke wrote the Acts and the chapters from 1 to 19 are a nightmare. It is mostly about Peter (the first Pope) that never seemed to understand what Jesus was about. The Holy Ghost has nothing to do with prophesy or speaking in tongues as it reads in the Acts 2:4. It is used for teaching the commandments of God to those that become saved only. St. John 14:15-26 says, "If ye love me, keep my commandments. And I will pray the Father, and he shall give you another Comforter, that (he) may abide with you forever; Even the Spirit of truth; whom the world cannot receive, because it seeth him not, neither knoweth him: but ye know him, for he dwelleth with you, and shall be in you. I will not leave you comfortless: I will come to you. Yet a little while, and the world seeth me no more; but ye see me, because I live ye shall live also. At that day ye shall know that I am in my Father, and ye in me, and I in you (December 1, 1968, at nine p.m.) But the Comforter, which is the Holy Ghost, whom the Father will send in my name, he shall teach you all things, and bring all things to your remembrance, whatsoever I have said unto you."

There are a lot of people that would die from believing in one verse of what Peter told mankind to do. Acts 2:38 says, "Then Peter said unto them, Repent, and be baptized every one of you in the name of Jesus Christ for the remission of sins, and ye shall receive the gift of the Holy Ghost. St. John 3:27 says, "John answered and said, A, am can receive nothing, except it be given him from heaven."

Mary

"And the angel came in unto her, (Mary) and said, Hail, thou that art highly favored, the Lord is with thee: blessed art thou among women" (St. Luke 1:28). In the thirty-fifth verse, it says, "The Holy Ghost shall come upon thee." St. Matthew got this wrong. Also, he said Mary was conceived by the Holy Ghost, but it was the other spirit. Was Mary a blessed mother? No. "For whosoever shall do the will of my Father which is in heaven, the same is my brother, and sister, and mother" (St. Matthew 12:50). Mark and St. John don't say anything about it.

The Catholic church puts a lot of their faith in Mary, from Luke, and they believe that St. John 6:53 justifies taking the Sacraments, but that verse has nothing to do with it.

What that verse means is receiving the born again experience and receiving the Holy Ghost, which is the only way to the kingdom of God, the way I received it. "Then Jesus said unto them, Verily, verily, I say unto you, Except ye eat the flesh of the Son of man, and drink his blood, ye have no life in you."

As I have said before, Ezekiel 36:26-25-27 happened to me physically. Jesus started out the Lord's prayer by saying, "Our Father which art in heaven." It doesn't say one word about praying to Mary. There is the one verse (above) that I go by that puts Mary as an equal to the common man. If she is saved, she must have received the same experiences as the rest of us by being born again and receiving the Holy Ghost. She had to wait until Jesus went to His Father after the crucifixion because the Holy Ghost wasn't to be until then. St. John 16:7 says, "Nevertheless I tell you the truth; It is expedient for you that I go away: for if I go (not) away, the Comforter will not come unto you; but if I depart, I will send him unto you." From Adam and Eve to Noah, was mankind any different that from Noah until today? It says that they were godless as they are today, and it says mankind would be the same when Jesus comes the second time, at the end of days. "But as the days of Noah (were), so shall also the coming of the Son of man be." St. Matthew 24:37 and 38 says, "For as in the days that were before the flood they were eating and drinking, marring and giving in marriage, until the day that Noah entered into the ark." Today, we have an eating establishment on every corner.

Love

Here is a verse that love is written into from man's and God's perspective. The Gospels never have love in it very many times, and it must be the preacher's favorite word. In St. John 15:12, "This is my commandment, That ye love one another, as I have loved you." Here it says, Jesus loves mankind and we are to love one another. What about these two verses after God created man? Genesis 6:5 says, "And God saw that the wickedness of man great in the earth, and that every imagination of the thoughts of his heart was only evil continually (all the day). And it repented (grieved) the Lord that he had made man on the earth, and it grieved him at his heart." Do you see what I'm getting at? God can't stand mankind, but He tells us "to love one another."

John 3:16 should not be in the KJB of 1611 as it is written. Verse 15 is a parable. When I was a child, they had me memorize 3:16, "For God so loved the world, that he gave his only begotten Son, that whosoever believeth in him (should) not perish, but have everlasting life." Someday added, "For God so loved the world," and instead of "eternal" they used "everlasting." The verse doesn't fit in with Genesis 6:6 above. If that is all there is, to just "believeth in him," the words "shall not perish" would have been used according to the rest of the Gospels. Eternal has a more precise meaning in the dictionary than everlasting.

Ben, who was my friend from the last trip, must have gotten my address from my ex-wife, of me living in San Pedro, California. He was knocking on the front door. I never went to the door because of the religious experience. I wasn't into drinking, women, and song as we were, when stationed on the ship, nor did I know how to explain it to him at the time.

It didn't take a rocket scientist to figure out that with the false doctrine in place throughout the religious community that I would have starved to death trying to change anybody's mind about their religion. The last twenty years I have tried, and it proved that I was correct, so I became a carpenter after I left California.

A year after changing the water or sensation in my body, I packed up everything I owned and put it in the Volkswagen with the child and dog. I went back home to Mom in Rapid city, South Dakota. When we arrived, she wasn't home, back it wasn't very long of a wait, and she got out of a taxicab.

Chapter 15

BACK HOME WITH MOM IN RAPID CITY, SOUTH DAKOTA

When Mom got out of the taxi, there was as much hate on her face as I had ever seen on a person. There were a few minutes when I didn't know if she was going to ask us to come in or not.

The prodigal son had returned, the one that had put every gray hair on her head, the on that slept all night in her bathroom on the floor, when he was home on leave in the navy. He couldn't help it that there was a layover in Denver, and he had to spend so much time in the bar. When I got to the house, Paul was sweating copper for the washing machine in her new washroom, and the wall caught on fire. With the navy training behind me, I pulled the Sheetrock off the wall to get at the fire. The bathroom floor, I needed it to sleep on that night, and sometime during the night, I moved from the floor to the bed. It was more comfortable.

She remembered the girl that was in my bed that I found at the carnival; when she got up for work at five a.m., she made me get up and take her to her parent's house. I'm not sure how she was, but after a frolic in the hay at her parent's house, she received a phone call from her mother. I said, "I'm not going to leave now. " A mile down the road, a police car came by with his lights and siren on. Her parents had been trying to find their daughter all night.

Mom had memories when I was just funning around, and after a while, she asked us to come in.

The first thing that I did was go downtown to an insurance agency to get insurance in South Dakota on the car. It was cheaper than California. Thirty days later, they asked me to come to their office, and the agent told me that they couldn't insure my car. I asked him why. He told me that I had a wreck in San Pedro, and I told him that at the time, I was lying on the couch. The ironic thing about this was the only wreck that I ever had was in 1955 on CY Street in Casper, Wyoming and the damage was only about one hundred fifty dollars when the police were called. I told Sis one time that there were a few hit and runs. After I was divorced and still in the navy, the same insurance the first time when I went in to pay my premium.

The next Sunday, I went to pay a Four Square Church because of the child. I certainly n ever had the same beliefs as they did and got a job painting houses at the Rapid City Air Force Base. With more men than suitable brushes, that never lasted forever, some painters were working on a building, and I went over to ask them if they needed any help. They told me to go to the paint store and talk to the owner. He asked me if I drank. I told him, "I don't even swear."

After he hired me, the next morning, the owner must have told the boss what I had said, and he was cussing up a storm, way over the top. I knew that I wasn't going to retire with that company. The first job, they put me with a journeyman painter, and he stained the garage door on the house, ate lunch, and went back to his business. I told the painter that I though the garage door needed another coat. He spray-painted it again, and the next day, the owner was blowing a fuse. He liked it with the one coat; he said it looked rustic.

They told me to go paint the new Cadillac garage on Omaha Street. It was rougher that a corncob. I'm not sure why they never spray-painted it. Every time the boss came by, I had to ask him for more paint. One gallon of paint only lasted about an hour, and they got rid of me after I finished painting it.

Mom saw a newspaper ad that said they were going to start a carpentry class at Stevens High School. They called it the Black Hills Area Vocational Technical School.

With my enrolment in place, I told Mom I would paint her house, and I signed up for the GI Bill benefit, which was between $100 and $150 a month. It left me no choice but to live with Mom for another year. I wasn't coming home between five and six a.m. and she liked that.

When I was painting her house, if she thought that she had a problem and went to the store, she would always ask for the top banana. It embarrassed me.

Through a church member, I got a part-time job at a coin gasoline service station. The manager couldn't fix the gasoline pumps if something went wrong. They had to wait until I came to work.

There were three of us that started the carpentry class, and eight that joined later from the unemployment agency. At the time, I was hungry to learn because I had never made any real money in my life, and I could see the opportunity it presented, the other student voted me in to be on the student council, and I had to report any news to the rest of the class.

During the hour for lunch, I went to the library and studied about construction or math. It was seldom that I never knew an answer that the teacher asked, which made me an A student. It was resented by some of the other students, and on a new garage that we built, someone slid a bundle of roofing off the roof. They knew I was putting the siding on below, and it could have broken my neck or killed me.

One of Dad's friends in Casper called me and said, "Your dad is about to die. His nose has been bleeding for days and he is drunk. We just took him to the hospital. Perhaps you should come over here."

Because he was in the hospital, I decided not to go. The doctor told him that if he didn't stop drinking, he would die. To my knowledge, that was the last big drunk that he ever went on. Sis and Merlyn always dropped everything on a moment's notice and went to him. I didn't, and that might have had something to do with his remaining sober.

Coming home from school one day, the dog, Lady, that I had bought in California was lying in the utility room. She had been run over in the street in front of the house. The next d ay, a young man knocked on the door and told Mom that the driver of the car had swerved over on the side of the road to run over the dog. After several days in the utility room, she got all right.

At the end of the year, I was selected to go to a special dinner, given by the Kiwanis Organization.
There was one contractor that came to the school, and the teacher told him I was his best student. He offered to pay me $2.75 an hour to run his company. I declined.

A motel owner hired me to remodel two of his motels.

When I told Dad what I was doing, he said, "One time, you told me you were afraid of working high off the ground."

Dad told me that they needed carpenters in Casper, Wyoming, and that I could live in his old green trailer that he had been living on for at least twenty years. He had bought a new Kirkwood trailer that was much bigger, at least ten feet wide and twenty-nine feet long.

We moved the trailer from one of his friend's house to the Riverside Mobile Home Court at 1250 North Center. I said I would like to live in a better location. It was a shock to him, as he had to lived there over twenty years, but it wasn't the first time that I shocked him.

Chapter 16

BACK IN CASPER, WYOMING

The first thing I had to do was pass the test or a journeyman carpenter. I missed one question, about a rabbit plane that they used several years back.

The business agent sent me to the Dave Johnston Power Plant, and Dad gave me an old-looking leather nail belt that he had used. He never wanted me looking like a little greenhorn. The work consisted of building forms for concrete, which we talked a little about in the carpenter class, but I had never actually made forms before. When I got home the first day, Dad asked me if I got a good job. I told him I wouldn't know one when I saw it.

The job lasted about four months for me, and then sent me to a uranium plant that made yellow cake, about fifty miles from Casper. The first day on the job, they gave me a pair of new had-toed work shoes. That evening, I showed Dad my new shoes, the second time in my life. The first was bought from the Salvation Army. And he said he never got a pair of brogans that I never seen him wear. They were huge and heavy. About six months later, Dad was sent out to the same job. The company never gave him any shoes because they said he was only hired temporarily.

The first time that I went inside the old green trailer, Dad handed me a small lamp and he told me to take it with me wherever I went. I put an electric light in each room, with a switch. After getting home from work, the breakfast dishes left in the sink there was no water trap that kept the sewer gas out of the sink and trailer. There was a lot of dried blood inside from nosebleeds that he had in the past. I cleaned it up as much as I could.

The mice were talking over the place, so I bought some traps, the spring-loaded some traps, the spring-loaded kind, and set one of them behind the door under the sink, and I placed one on the floor. When I got home from work, I opened the door and mouse jumped from the shelf to the floor. It handed right on the middle of the trap and that wasn't pretty. The other trap already had a mouse in it.

After living in it about two months, I went over to Dad's trailer and told him that I had to move out. He asked what was the matter. Black soot was driving me out of the house. It was even on the cobwebs. He came over to the trailer and pulled down a hidden door inside the furnace. He had hooked up the fuel oil barrel to the furnace, but I lit the pilot light and didn't know about the hidden door.

In about six months, I mentioned that the water from the hot water tank was too hot water. He said "I only plug it in when I need hot water." I'm not sure how I lived so long around that man.

One day, he came over to the trailer and told me the Yamaha dealer had two red motorcycles for sale for $500. He said that he would buy one if I bought the other. My life savings at the time was one thousand dollars, and it would take half of my life savings so I declined. He went ahead and bought one of the motorcycles. When he took it back to the

158

dealer to get the braking-in oil replaced, he drove it off the lot. I'm not sure when he noticed the engine getting hot, but they forgot to put any oil back in it, after they drained it. I would have taken it back and gave it to them, but they put in it, and he drove it home.

It was about thirty below zero when I drove past Dad at his trailer from the job. He had the hood up on his truck. I walked over and asked him what he was doing. He said, "I'm trying to start it."

So I asked him, "Where are you going if you get it started?"

He told me, "No place."

Then to show me what ether can do, he sprayed the entire can into the carburetor. The truck started, but it ruined the engine. He went to the Ford garage for an estimate to have it repaired, but they couldn't tell him exactly what the problem was, so he traded it in for a Chevrolet truck with automatic shift, which he should have had since he was born the automatic shift that is.

He had two daughters from one of his girlfriends in the fifties, and we were going to go up on Casper Mountain for a picnic. When we got in the back of the truck, one of his daughters got in the front seat with him. The other got in the back with my son and I. he drove about thirty feet and slammed on the brake. We all went toward the back of the cab, with the toolboxes and loose tools and etc.

Dad and his two daughters went up on Casper Mountain another time after he bought four new tires. On the way back to town, he noticed something was wrong. He stopped and got out. None of the lug nuts were tightened; they had only put them on finger tight. He had to have all the lug bolts replaced, and that happened to me one time, when I forgot to tighten the nuts as a teenager.

When he bought his new trailer, the dealer offered to hook up the utilities, but Dad told them he could do it. He hooked up the water to the natural gas line, and it damaged his appliances and furnace.

He went to Gillette, Wyoming, to work on a schoolhouse, and the construction had just started. I about a week, I went down to eat in a restaurant on a Friday evening, and Dad was sitting in a booth. You could have knocked me over with a feather. I sat down and he said, "You know, Mick, I saw some ducks flying south, and that's where I'm going."

In a couple of days, he asked me if I would buy his new trailer, and because of the water capper, I told him no. about a week went by, and he told me that he sold the trailer that I was living in, and that I would have to move out. He sold it to a sheep herder that had just gotten married, but his wife wouldn't live in it, and I'm not sure what happened to the old green trailer.

In the *Casper Journal*, there was an advertisement to sell a trailer that had an expanded front room. It was comfortable, and I lived in it about thirteen years.

A year after moving to Casper from Rapid City, they had a six-inch rain. In one of the meteorology classes at Casper

College, the professor said that the flood was caused by cloud seeding. The flood happened at midnight, and I went there the same day. Mom managed to hold on to a chest of drawers that saved her life because the water got up to six feet inside the house. Several of her neighbors were drowned, and I believe two hundred thirty-seven people lost their lives. Most of the neighborhood houses either were gone or not repairable.

Mom managed to rent a house in Rapid City. She knew that her house could be repaired, and eventually, she would move back in it. When I got to her house, a woman gave me Mom's new address, and not long afterward, Sis and Merlyn came from Cuba City, Wisconsin. We shoveled mud out of the windows and removed the muddy carpet. There were dead fish in the kitchen. The next day I went back to Casper, Wyoming, because of my carpenter job.

One if the ironic things that happened was Mom had been taking driver's training and had just received a driver's license. That same day of the flood, she bought a Dodge Swinger and gassed it up before parking it in a three-sided garage at the back of her house. Nine hours later, the flood destroyed the car. She could have driven a car her entire life, as long as it was an automatic shift. Her left leg was damaged because of polio, and she never drove a car again.

Mom hired Dad to come over from Casper to work on the house for twenty dollars an hour cash. At the time, he was not working and I was. He couldn't seem to understand that the house would eventually be bought by the government. He could have saved a lot of money by buying cheaper materials, hollow core doors instead of solid for instance. When Dad was finished with the rough work, I didn't have a job, so I went from Casper to Rapid City to do the finish work. I put linoleum over one inch of rigid insulation on the kitchen countertop. The government bought whatever you had on the lot, and most people, all they had was the lot, which they never received much money for.

The only thing I lost was a collection of the forties and fifties records that was in the living room. The large plate glass window had gotten broken, and when the water receded out the window, it sucked my vinyl records out.

At first, Dad moved into the house until they got in an argument over a trivial matter, and then he moved out in a shed with a dirt floor at the back of the lot, next to the three-sided garage.

One day, they were scheduled to go to the lumberyard for materials. When Dad went out towards his truck, he noticed that he had a flat tire. He jacked up the truck to put the spare on, and when Mom arrived by taxicab, she opened the passenger side door of the cab but couldn't get in. Dad was sitting under the steering wheel and told her that she had been getting in the truck. Then he remembered that he jacked up the truck to get the spare tire on, and the jack was still holding the
truck up in the air. Mom said, "You put the spare tire on, on my time."

The day that I moved my things over to the trailer that I bought, Dad had a new truck and drove past me several times without asking me if I needed any help. I moved everything over with a 1969 VW, including a boat trailer that I bought from him for fifty dollars, just to be nice.

He sold his new trailer to a carpenter that he worked with in Gillette, as is. What that meant was TV, dish rags, towels, silverware, soap, dish soap, laundry soap, toilet paper, etc., everything but his shoes and clothes.

He went to Miller, Missouri, and bought five acres with a small house on it. He told his lady friend to clean the trailer up for the new owner, and two years later, he told me he saw a lot of things in her house that he sold with the trailer. She must have thought he said, "Clean it out for the new owner."

Remember, Dad was the preacher and Paul was the farmer. He stocked his farm with barn animals that he said ate him out of house and home. He added a room to the back of the house, and I never did see his farm. He eventually bought a lot in Springfield, Missouri, and built a house on it with old bricks that he acquired from another building that he tore down. Paul asked me, "Why did Dad do such a poor job laying the bricks in Springfield, and he did such a nice job in Rapid City?"

I told him, "He never laid the blocks in Rapid City. Mister Coon did that, who sold him the half-finished house and lot."

In the wintertime, I would go ice fishing and put my fishing equipment on a sled that my son had never played with that I got him for Christmas. I would always go on the lake on a Monday. I never had to drill a h ole and used somebody else's ice hole that they drilled over the weekend.

At that time, half of the beer was in bottles with a cap that you had to take off. I mentioned to Sis if she remembered the time Dad drove from Casper, Wyoming, to visit her in Cuba City, Wisconsin, and she said she did. When he got to her house, he told Merlyn that he couldn't go very fast in his VW. Merlyn went out to his car and came back in the house with a beer bottle cap that had gotten wedged under the gas pedal. Sis said that he drove six hundred miles that way.

Chapter 17

WORKING AS A CARPENTER

The best way to start out as a carpenter, I believe, is the way I did it, by enrolling in a vocational school. It can happen that if you go through an apprentice program, you can get stuck in one segment of the carpenter trade. The second job, I was teamed up with another carpenter, and the boss put us on scaffolding, which neither of us had ever done before; we had to learn on the job. The man that I worked with was a hard worker, but that never did scare me. What was unique about it was the laborer that they gave us. He only had one hood arm; the other one hung straight down, and very few people knew about his handicap. He did his work to our satisfaction, so we never considered it as handicap. He was a bull moose as far as strength went, with the one arm.

The third job was in another uranium plant, and I was the lead carpenter doing scaffolding for the other trades. One morning, going to the job about six miles from Casper, it had rained all night, and what was usually a dry creek bed had become a torrent of water going over the road. The VW engine stalled in a creek, and a man came by with a four-wheel drive truck. With a rope attached, he pulled me to the jobsite. The engine was ruined, and the insurance company determined that because of the mileage on the engine, it was only good for a few more miles, so they gave me fifty dollars in damages.

For the next thirteen years, I worked for various contractors. One of the jobs stands out, the La Prele Dam; it was about forty miles from Casper. It was spring, and in

Wyoming, the bad weather can get worse than that. From the highway to the jobsite, the VW couldn't get through the snow. Another carpenter lived in Casper that drove a four-wheel drive truck. I asked him if I could ride with him, and he picked me up in the morning and took me home.

One day it was snowing, and he came over where I was working. He asked me if I would go back to Casper with him. I told him they would probably shut the job down. And everybody would leave. The third time, I told him I would leave. We were walking toward his truck, and the main superintendent drove up beside us. He told us that he had been looking for a couple of carpenters to lay off and that we were as good as any, and he told us to go over to the trailer and get our money. That was the last time that I ever rode with anyone. The job lasted at least a year after that.

Not long afterward, I took a used 1971 four-wheel drive Jeep Wagoner for a test drive, and after they fixed the leaking gas tank, I bought it.

During those thirteen years, I lived modestly in a trailer without spending nearly what I was earning, and every time I got one thousand dollars in the bank, I would get a CD or money market certificate. We were getting 12 to 16 percent interest on our savings, the interest rate is .20, .25, and the best interest on a CD that I could find was .50 percent. It is criminal, and I told my bank that I was going to call the sheriff.

As a protest, I left what little money I have in my checking account, and I asked the teller what the bank does with the money in the checking accounts? She said she didn't know.

166

The Events Center in Casper was the last major job that I did as a union carpenter.

In Casper, Wyoming, there were about three thousand government properties for sale in the newspaper. The prices were down where I lived, and I could pay cash for most of them. I borrowed a limited amount but always kept it at a minimum. Any sign of trouble, either real estate or credit cards, I could pay them off if they raised the interest rate, etc. It wasn't until I was about fifty years old that I got my first credit card from American Express for the three hundred dollars a year, and that opened up a flood of credit card requests for me.

Chapter 18

REAL ESTATE
ENTREPRENEUR

The first house that I bought was an estate bank-owned small house to live in. they opened the bids, and I was the highest bidder. The bank offered the house to lower bidders, asking them if they would go over the bid that I offered. No one offered them more money, so I was given the house, and I never thought that was fair, but I'm only a carpenter that just barely made it through high school. I paid cash for the house.

My son had finished two years of college without a degree, and I couldn't remember him bringing home a book in high school or college. He took piano lessons six years until the teacher finally told him he should take up shoeing horses.

It had been fifteen years since o had a date with a woman, and my son said that he would like to go to Texas to live with his mother. "All my ex's lived in Texas."

We had been going to the United Pentecostal Church, and the reason for that was the child. They believed that when you baptized a person in water, you automatically are saved and receive the Holy Ghost (Acts 2:38), which is a farce. What about what the rest of the Bible has to say in regard to salvation? The women in the church were either under twelve or over sixty years old, and at the time, I was about thirty-five.

When my son left, I put an advertisement in the newspaper: "Wanted, a woman over eighteen, and money wouldn't be a problem." One woman that answered the ad was a police officer wife that only wanted sex. There were only about six that answered the ad, with three dates.

Edna sent me a letter, and I decided to make a date with her. She seemed okay, and we decided that she would quit renting where she was at, and I would sell the trailer that I was living in. we moved into the house that I bought from the bank together. Love of one another was never an issue. That was the way it had to be with me because I loved the Lord my God with all my heart, soul, and mind. It never left any extra love for anybody else on earth. In the King James Bible of 1611, prove me wrong in the Gospels of St. John, Matthew, Mark, and the Old Testament. You probably can, but that is your problem. The Bible says that, "Wherefore they are no more twain, but one fish, what therefore God hath joined together, let not man put asunder." Does it say anything about a preacher putting them together? "Thy kingdom come thy will be done in earth as it is in heaven. The children of this world marry, and are given in marriage: But they which shall be accounted worthy to obtain that world, and the resurrection from the dead, neither marry, nor are given in marriage." "Neither can they die any more: for they are equal unto the angels; and are the children of God, being the children of the resurrection. For when they shall rise from the (dead) they neither marry, nor are given in marriage; but are as the angels which are in heaven." (I died than rose again (or was reborn or made alive) when God transferred the heart that I was born with, and gave me a heart from God here on this earth.) Psalm 119:40 says "Behold, I have longed after thy precepts: (laws) quicken (make alive) me in thy righteousness. He that over cometh shall not be hurt of the second death." Revelation 2:11 says, "Thou shalt love the Lord thy God with all thy heart, and with all thy soul, and with all thy mind. This is the first and great commandment. For thou shalt worship no other God: for the Lord, whose name is Jealous, is a jealous God." Could this mean what it says, that we can get into trouble with God if you put anything or anybody first in your life or whatever is your idol.

The only thing that I can do is tell you what seemed to work for me in regard to marriage and show you verses that pertained to it. If you are young and in the reproductive age, with children involved, perhaps you can be married in a civil ceremony. That might work for you. You must remember that it would put you under the laws of man, but if it works for you, that is what is important. If it was me, I would hesitate being married in a church. The first thing they tell you is how qualified they are to perform the ceremony. I don't mean to imply that death is the same as being married, but one of the disciples told Jesus that he needed to go and bury his father. But Jesus said unto him, "Follow me, and let the (dead) bury their dead" (St. Matthew 8:22). It tells me that the preachers in the churches haven't been made alive by seeing born again nor received the Holy Ghost, as I found both are real and physical.

I'm aware that on this earth, there is no subject that can condemn me any quicker by the masses, but be careful, for you might be wrong and I'm right.

Most of the houses that I bought were not livable. Every one of them took different amounts of money for repairs. When I bought a house or duplex, I would rent or sell the house and use the money for repairs on the next investment. For all practical purposes, I retired when I was fifty years old. At least I could do whatever I wanted to do at any time; that could be the definition of retirement.

According to most of the flippers, as they have become known, or entrepreneurs, most of them will tell you to borrow money until your eyeballs are dropping out of their sockets. I never did it that way. All I wanted was enough money to live on and stay out of trouble.

Fixing the houses, I did almost all the work myself. I never was afraid of work.

The buyers and renters are the real story in this book. It is college education in human relations.

The second single-family house that I bought, I rented it at first, and when they moved out. I put it up for sale. I doubled the money with a contract for deed, which means that a bank keeps all the papers, pays the insurance, property taxes, and the bank collects the monthly proceeds. They deposit the money in my checking account, which most of it went to repair my last investment. The garage was a double-car garage that you could drive in from the alley or the front.

It wasn't very long, and the buyer inherited some money when a relative died in Montana. He paid off the contract for deed, so I had money for investing.

One day, he knocked on my door and told me the house burned down. He said it was cold, and he worked on repairing car parts in the basement. He said that he threw his gasoline-soaked rags in a bucket, and that is not a good idea. Gasoline, in a confirmed space, will create heat from the gasoline-soaked rags, and if you give it enough time, it will start a fire. He had insurance and replaced it with a prefabricated house.

My next investment was a duplex. I fixed up one side and advertised it for rent in the local paper. It was more than thirty days when I got a young unmarried couple to rent it. At the end of the month, we got a snowstorm. The lady told her boyfriend that it was the landlord's job to come over and shovel the walk. He told her it wasn't his job. She got mad and moved out. With half of the rent payment gone, he couldn't pay all the rent, so he had to leave also.

The third house that I bought, the real estate lady and I had a flashlight to inspect the house. The batteries must have been low. It took a lot of money for repairs, and when I finished it, I put an advertisement in the newspaper to sell.

A woman showed up barefoot, and the couple bought it, contract for deed.

In about a year, they had gotten behind a couple months on their payment and let the fire insurance expire. Tuesday, I went over to the house, and Danny told me he was getting a divorce and had filed for bankruptcy. He also told me that he got lead poisoning from chewing on a pencil while he was laying carpet. I told him that the least thing that he could do was get the fire insurance reinstated.

The next Saturday, I got a phone call that my house on Lowell was burning down. I had just talked to the fire inspector and told him the guy who was buying the house was a loose cannon. The loose cannon came walking up, as flames were shooting out of the roof. I asked him if he had gotten any insurance. He said "Yes, yesterday."

He had not slept in the house that night, and the fish were removed from the fish tank. Several days before, he had noticed the lights becoming dim and had sensed that it was going up in smoke. The fire inspector determined it was an electrical fire. The insurance company paid me off, and Danny had enough money from his personal property to rebuild it. I'm not sure why he built in on the original foundation because it leaked water in the basement, which was made out of cement blocks.

On two occasions when I was working on two different rentals, after getting back from the lumberyard, I was locked out of the houses because of sex. One of them was the daughter, who was only sixteen years old, and before I had left, her boyfriend from school had arrived. The other couple moved the furniture a block on their back, and I decided then that I would never put a For Rent sign in the window again. It's better to get a renter from across town, if you know what I mean.

One day, I had a problem with the front door, and when I came back from the lumberyard, they had me locked out. I could hear them in the bed, through the window. I'm just glad it only lasted about three minutes.

After renting a one-bedroom apartment to a couple from California, they asked me if would fix a minor settling crack in the bathroom. Several times, they told me that the husband had to go back to California tomorrow morning. I

173

told them I would be over in the morning to fix the crack. When I knocked on the door, she said, "Come in," and when I went in, she was lying on a mattress in the living room, with a very little on but the radio. I walked past her to the bathroom with the joint compound and tools. In about five minutes, her husband came through the front door, who was supposed to be on his way to California. Whatever they had on their mind, I couldn't tell you.

The majority of the renters were evicted for one reason or another. One of them, after they left, I flipped the light switch on in each room, and it was the same—nothing happened. They had removed every light bulb, including the two porch lights.

Another one turned the main electrical breaker switch off in the middle of winter. If I hadn't gone over there soon after they left, it could have frozen water lines. I had the opportunity to ask him why he did that. He said that was the way it was when he moved in.

I found out everybody liked to live in a park, as long as somebody else maintains it. One took my lawn mower when they have now it when I pay the water bill.

A woman, who had a fourteen-year-old son, rented a house, and I left a lawn mower with her. I told the son that it used a little oil, and I showed him how to check the oil. I went by the house a few days later, and the grass hadn't been mowed. I went around to the back of the house, and the lawn mower was where I had left it. Her son had poured the quart of oil over the entire outside of the engine. What do you do when a renter in a duplex, whom you would like to get rid of, recommends his friend to rent the other side

174

when it becomes empty? After renting it to him, he paid two months' rent, which was different. It was the last money that he ever gave me. When I asked a friend of his about him after he left, he told me that he
had just got out of the penitentiary. Before he left, he took a chair and slammed it into the wall and broke the Sheetrock.

I left my mother's bedroom set in a rental, and the guy fell in love with another man in Denver. He gave the key to his brother. His brother sold everything in the house that he could and left. The rest of their stuff I took to the dump, and a few days later, their mother called me up to ask me what I did with the pictures. That was sad.

A renter that worked at a bank broke five windows in two months.

I never liked a lease because the renter can move out at any time, and I can evict them at any time. That suits me just fine, but if there are children involved, I have to be extra careful with them. Some of them would leave for one reason or another in about one month.

The last vacancy that I had, I had an application to fill out. Of course, I chose the wrong couple. I explained to him that there was an eighty-year-old lady in the apartment below, and I was looking for someone a little quiet. She had just left the hospital. That must have gone over his head because the other half of the rent was due on Friday. Saturday at four-thirty a.m., I got a call that the renter below had to call the police because there was so much noise.

I arrived shortly after the police had left, and going up to the door, there was a glass all over the stairway. Going in the house, there was a three-year-old boy that was not on the application; only baby was mentioned. The range door was open, with the oven coils red hot for heat. I'm not sure why, as the apartment had natural gas and electric heaters. The front door had been kicked in, and he was trying to pay the rest of the rent that was due at midnight, but it was four-thirty a.m. I wouldn't accept the payment. I told him that he had to leave, but if he left in five days, I would give the money back that he gave me originally.

What I understood was they got into an argument moving in, between midnight and five a.m. he was driving nails in the walls, and he never broke the window. That only left his wife or three-year-old son who did that. This all happened a few days before Christmas.

On the fifth day, I got a call that he needed the money I promised for the moving van. I told him that I would be right over. When I got there, his wife pointed out the new floor that they had put in, he had gone to the store of some kind, purchased twelve-inch square self-sticking tile, one-sixteenth-inch thick, and put them over the linoleum. He never put the new tile under the baseboard, and at the last wall, he laid the tile o top of the new tile, instead cutting it to fit. He did all this after I told him he had to leave.

After I decided to rent the same apartment with the new floor the way it was, I got a one-hundred-dollar deposit from a single lady, and she never contacted me again.

Another woman with a small child, at a different rental, told me if I would put a gate between the shed and the house, that she would rent it. She never moved in, and the gate never been used.

Renting an apartment to a schoolteacher never turned out very well. Dad had just knocked on the door for a visit, and I got a frantic call from the teacher's wife; she couldn't get the water to shut off in the bath tub. I went over and shut the water off; she was trying to turn the knob to the wrong way. She was so embarrassed that they moved out at the end on the month. All I said was "I'm glad that was all that's wrong. My dad just came for a visit."

Another time, I was called over to an apartment at three a.m. the woman wouldn't stop singing. She and I had just signed a government contract paying part of the lease that expired in a year. The next day, I asked her if she would leave and that I wouldn't tell the agent that she liked to sing at three a.m. Surprisingly, she said yes. My next step was going to the government agent. I told her that the tenant and I had agreed on a no-fault divorce to break the lease.

The tenants have to put the natural gas and electricity in their name, usually by cell phone, with me present, when they first rented it.

One man came to look at the apartment with his mother. She asked me to paint the kitchen cabinets, which I did. He paid for one-month rent, let the natural gas go back into my name, and left.

This past summer, I reroofed a duplex, and it was either raining or snowing. The wooden back screen door of one of the apartments swelled shut, so the tenant said he hit the screen door with his shoulder. He never turned the knob, and it tore out the latch and a good part of the door.

Two of the tenants liked my apartments so much, I had to get the sheriff to evict them. I asked the judge for a restraining order against one of them because he carried a hatchet. The judge told me that wasn't his apartment. The other one, I asked his mother if she could do something, and she told me to call the sheriff. A few years later, he was a cook in a small café that made me a rib-eye dinner, and all I could do was hope he never recognized me.

A woman lived in a single-family house for ten years and recently moved out. Somehow, the door to the dishwasher became broken and wouldn't close. She never did tell me about it but continued using it. When I pulled it out of the kitchen cabinets, it almost knocked me to my knees with the smell. The only time that she ever called me when she had a problem was when the inside of her driver was on fire. The fire department said they had never heard of a drier catching fire in that way; it was one of the controlling switches. I thought a renter wouldn't call me even if their house was burning down, but she proved me wrong.

Chapter 19

LIFE AFTER PUBERTY

What makes me disgusted with what is going on in the Middle East is the way the rucks got started in the first place. In the Casper Star Tribune, we have what is known as the Answer Girl. Anybody can ask a question on any topic, and most of the time, they try to give you an answer. I asked her this question, "What was the reason that Iraq attacked Kuwait in the first place?" My brother was given the same question. He said it was over oil. The Answer Girl said it was over oil, and she said that was what the archives had recorded in Washington, DC. If it was over oil, then why did Hussein light the oil wells on fire? Wasn't that more of a punishment on Kuwait than anything else? Anyone with a half of a brain would know that the United States wouldn't stand by and watch Iraq take over Kuwait without getting involved. Iraq never had much of anything to fight a war with in Desert Storm.

We may have been the instigator of why Iraq used the limited supply of chemicals on the Kurds because a lot of people thought the United States was going to go after Hussein in the Desert Storm War, which we probably should have. If nothing else, for the crime against humanity of setting the oil wells on fire. We will never know how many Iraq people were killed because we packed our bags at the border and went home.

Hussein was captured in a spider hole during the second was and went to trial, and the verdict was to hang him. Before he was hung, he talked to one journalist, Mr.

George. What he told him sounded like two drunks in a bar, but truth is stranger than fiction.

Printed out from the internet, a CBS News report on January 27, 2008, is information that there was one man George Piro, working for the FBI and CIA. Saddam Hussein called him Mr. George. There is six pages to the report, but I will only mention one item. That invasion was in 1990. Back then, Saddam accused Kuwait of wrecking Iraq's economy by stealing oil and demanding repayment of loans. But Mr. George learned, for the first time, that the brutal invasion was triggered by personal insult.

What really triggered it for him, according to Saddam, was he had sent his foreign minister to Kuwait to meet with the Emir Al-Sabah, the former leader of Kuwait, to try to resolve some of these issues. And the Emir told the foreign minister of Iraq that he would not stop doing what he was doing until he turned every Iraqi woman into a $10 prostitute. And that really sealed it for him to invade Kuwait. Mr. George explained that he wanted to punish the Emir Al-Sabah for saying that.

After the two trade centers were bombed by nineteen men in two airplanes from Saudi Arabia, the United States found out their leader was living in Afghanistan. With over three thousand people that died, as they say, vengeance is mine. The men came from a good oil producer, Saudi Arabia, and I don't believe that country was ever a target. With a mild war raged at first with Afghanistan, what I understand is the better targets were in Iraq, and Hussein said the president's dad would like to kill him. It sounds like another story that you might hear down at the local bar, but it had a lot to do with the eventual war with Iraq the second time.

The inspectors that went in to inspect for chemicals or other armaments told our government that Hussein never had anything to be concerned about.

Hussein said before he was hung that he only pretended to have chemical weapons to keep the neighboring countries scared of Iraq. That was why the chickens where deployed to the front lines. They would die before the US Marines. My dad told me in the underground mines that they used canaries as their defense against bad gas.

I read in the newspaper the other day, a letter to the editor by Al Hamburg, that the Vietnam War was started from a lie, that a North Vietnam patrol boat attacked a US Navy shup in the Gulf of Tonkin. Several years later, Congress ruled it was a lie, but the Vietnam War went on for years and 58,000 US troops died. I was stationed on a navy ship six years bringing in supplies and cargo. You never heard of a ship being fired on because a lot of supplies were black-marketed to the enemy, I was told.

It wasn't long after Russia left Afghanistan that the Soviet Union came apart, and I believe it had a lot to do with it. It was not a sufficient reason for the United States to try and avoid getting mired down in a country, that to my knowledge has never been defeated as far back as their history goes. I voted for Obama, but when he was running for office, the one thing that I couldn't understand is why he wanted to continue the fight there.

One day at the post office, I had mailed a package, and the lady asked me, "Do you want any stamps?"

"No," I said. "I bought five hundred dollars' worth of forever stamps, and when they run out, I'm going to die.

She said, "Well, I hope it works out for you."

Last September, I was driving back from Colorado Springs with my sister for a visit to Casper, Wyoming. We stopped at a truck stop, and we were looking at the menu, gravy was mentioned between us. When the waitress came to take our order, my sister said she wanted the roast beef. The waitress said, "Do you want the hardy meal?"

"Yes," she said, "with a lot of gravy. I'm hungry."

I told her to give me the same. When our meal was placed before us, it was hard to believe. I started eating as if there was nothing wrong, and not far into the meal, Sis said, "Are you going to eat all that?"

The roast beef was overcooked, also shredded, and it looked like there were two pounds on each plate, with gravy halfway up on the beef and mashed potatoes. We started laughing and couldn't stop until I decided to ask for a doggie bag. The waitress came with a box that she put the leftovers in and said it will make a nice sandwich tomorrow. Sis was in a
wheelchair, and I paid at the cash register. When we were outside, I asked her where the box was.

When I was in the navy in San Francisco, there were four of us that went in a Chinese restaurant. They sensed that we were drunk and wouldn't serve us. They were probably right.

I was in a bar, in uniform, in Rapid City, and an Indian man had his head lying on top of the counter in his arms. A woman came in and started hitting him over the head with a beer bottle. I stood up after I couldn't take it anymore. The bartender came around where I was at and threw me out the door. I was about to leave anyway.

In Casper, I ordered pork chops and eggs. They had cut the pork chops out of a pork roast to make them look like pork chops.

Last night, at another restaurant, I ordered a rib-eye steak dinner, medium rare. They brought a small piece of sirloin steak with a little dab of vegetables. The steak was overcooked, with no bread or choice of soup or salad. They had the price if what a normal rib-eye dinner would cost. On the way out, they opened the door for us. I have had a lot of bartenders open the door for me, but this was the first time it happened in a restaurant.

In Omaha, Nebraska, I went to steakhouse restaurant by myself, and the hostess took me past twenty-five empty tables to a table next to the bathroom. Later, one of the cooks and I stated talking. I asked him, "Why did the hostess bring me all the way back here?" He told me I looked like trouble.

In Laramie, Wyoming, for an evening meal, I ordered pork chops. The waitress asked me, "What do you want on you lettuce?"

At least, they were honest, but the pork chops I sent back to the kitchen. The first time in my life.

They were saying on the TV to take alternative routes because of all the road construction in town. Evidently, the police weren't watching TV or were they, because on my left, coming out of the mall, it looked like a battle zone. I drove across the road from the mall, and in about a block, I saw a squad car sitting on a corner, and as I went past him, the police car started to move. It came up behind me, and I couldn't figure out what I did wrong. At the window, the cop said that it was against the law to cross the road from the mall. On the back of the ticket, there was a telephone number that I needed to call to find out how much the offense was. It turned out to be fifty dollars, and on the ticket, it said to mail it to this address. The next day, I mailed the fifty dollars in an envelope to the courthouse, across the street from the post office. It had always worked before, and I was no stranger to getting tickets.

About a month later, I was driving down first street and turned on Durbin. I had just passed a police car in the other lane, and it came up behind me. He flashed his lights and before I got the car stopped, it was partially on the sidewalk before I could get my seat belt fastened. I couldn't figure out what the offense was. The window never worked, so I opened the door, and he told me to put the knife in the door panel and throw it in the back seat. The police officer told me that there was a warrant out for my arrest because I never paid a fine. I told him I paid that fine the next day and sent it to the courthouse. He said that wasn't under his jurisdiction.

In the meantime, his backup arrived and got in the 1977 Buick Century that never needed a key and moved it off the sidewalk. For several years, I had used the back seat and passenger side for trash. When he got out of the car, he just shook his head. The police officer handcuffed me, and I told him that this was the first time I was ever handcuffed. He asked me if I had any money and that I would need $750 for a bond. I told him I had that much across the street, that was my bank. When we got over to side entrance of the bank, he took the handcuffs off so I could get the cash money out. He put me in a wire cage in the back seat of his squad car and took me to the police station. I asked him how I was going to get back to my car. He told me he would stay with me and bring me back.

Inside the station, a pretty policewoman counted the money several times in front of me, and I kept my mouth shut. She had a peashooter on her hip. It looked better on her hip than the officer that arrested me. They took my picture and information that I wouldn't give to my mother. After I said it was time for lunch, the officer took me back to my car. On the way, I called my friend on the cell phone to tell her that I managed to get my seat belt fastened, and I was riding in a cage in a police car. When we were about three blocks from my car, the police officer told me he was a preacher. At my court hearing, I couldn't believe the judge would take up so much time on my case. I proved that I sent the money in with my checkbook. The judge told me that he could fine me $750. He fined me the original fifty dollars, but what I couldn't understand was he said I was under some kind of probation for nine months. I followed the rules to the best of my ability, so what was the nine months' probation for? The way I understood it if I screwed up on those nine months, I would have to pay the $750 plus whatever the fine was for the next ticket.

First of all, it was on an Indian reservation. I believe it was called the Wind River Campgrounds between Casper and Thermopolis, Wyoming. It was on a Saturday, and there had been road construction, perhaps during the previous week. Most of the construction signs were pushed over, and going down the hill to the first campground, a pickup truck was parked on the side road waiting for me. When I got to the pickup, it pulled out in front of me and I went on past it. In about a block, I looked in my rearview mirror, and there was one red flashing light just above the bumper on the driver's side. Pulling over to the side of the road and stopping, a woman got out of the pickup wearing blue jeans, with a pea shooter on her hip. She said, "You went past me in a no passing zone."

If there was another car within ten miles, I would have been surprised, as this happened in Wyoming. I must have said something distasteful because she said, "We are in a work zone, and you could be fined double."

After sending the money in, the Indians probably got half of it, and I forgot all about it. The car was insured, and the next time my premium came due, it had on there that I received a ticket (the first one in nine years) and your premium has increased (almost double) for the next three years.

The last time that I had an accident was in 1955 in Casper, Wyoming. The damage to the other car was about $150. That was when money was worth something. Needless to say, I went
to another insurance company, and they told me what they did to me was criminal with one ticket.

In 1982, I had bought a house and finished the room above a separated double garage from the house. I never could get any fire insurance on it. In 2002, I paid $40,000 down on another house, and they would only insure it for the amount of what I owed on the mortgage. An insurance company goes by what the square foot replacement company sent me a letter that they couldn't insure my old houses for the replacement cost, but they put a set value on each one of them.

In real estate, what sells books are those that tell you to borrow money until your eyeballs drop out of their sockets. One book said to sell the shrubbery, flowers, and young trees for the down payment. I had to sell about four houses to pay the house off that I'm living in, in about ten months. Then if that isn't enough, the books that sell is when they say you can get a thirty-plus year loan. The advantage is, look at all the tax deductible money you can save on your income taxes. A lot of people could pay the house off in fifteen years or less, and some could even do better than that, but they say, "Who me? And lose all that deductible advantage on my taxes, you're crazy."

Thirty years is a long time; just think of all that could happen in those many years. The company could go to Mexico or China. I have often said that you had to be as dumb as the boss. What if in ten years, you never matched up or measured down. Let's say you took out the thirty-year loan when you were thirty-five and fooled around with the deductible advantages. Somewhere along the line, your job that you went to college for could have disappeared or went to India. God only knows, every time you get a divorce, the property is split in half. How many halves are you going to accumulate? Thirteen kids, with two divorces, and three marriages, like my brother. The pickup truck might be the only thing left that is yours.

Are you going to stay as healthy as you were when you took the loan out perhaps a drunk seventeen-year-old did you in, in his dad's car or a forty-year-old, after he just split another half, and was out celebrating. I believe I'm right about this, any mortgage, you can ask for a printout of your mortgage payments (amortization) and all you have to do is pay two principal payments and one interest payment, etc. in fifteen years, you can pay off a thirty-year loan. Or you could wait until one of the skits overtake you above and go whine to whomever wants to listen to you about the hardship you're under.

Toward the end of building the Events Center in Casper, Wyoming, I thought I would get a leg up on moving to another town for a carpenter job, so I bought a thirty-two-foot Holiday Rambler Travel Trailer. It was only about three years old, and the inside was beautiful. The problem that I had though, I was overseeing the care of my mother, and it looked like she wasn't going to live forever, but she did.

Dad came to Casper on a visit, and he was visiting with Mom and me inside house. After a while, Dad said, "Let's go out, and let me look at your trailer."

It was parked behind her house. I went inside first and Dad followed me. When I turned around to explain something to him, all I saw was his back going out the door. If I would have had about a sixteen-foot home made trailer, like the one he made when I was born, I believe he would have stayed.

That summer, mom and I decided to take a trip with it to the Black Hills of South Dakota. We stopped in Hot Springs, and I went swimming at the Star Plunge. I had been going there since I was fourteen years old when I lived in Rapid City, South Dakota. When we left there and went north through the Custer State Park, I saw a sign: Needles Highway. A girl in a booth took our fee to drive through. It wasn't until sometime later that I found out at the entrance, there was a sign that said, "No trailers allowed past this point," but I never noticed the sign. The girl never said anything but took the fee. It is part of my life history of finding man's inhumanity to man, except this time, it was a girl.

Down the road, I came upon a tunnel that was blasted through the rock, close to 1900, and with an air conditioner mounted on the top, I'm not sure how I got the trailer through it. At one point, I stopped the trailer in the middle with both lanes of traffic stopped. I got out and it looked like I had drove in the tunnel at a perfect angle to go on through. Only one running light was all that was broke. Down the road, I believe there were three more tunnels, but none of them were as small as the first one. I'm not sure why my mother never had a heart attack on that trip. There was another fiasco at Sylvia Lake, but

I pulled that one out also, after turning off at a campground that wasn't compatible for a trailer.

After being in the navy foe eight years, four years in Long Beach, and four years in San Diego, California, I was glad that I learned how to drive before last summer when I went to Los Angeles from Casper, Wyoming. Somehow I managed to get the car back in one piece. Going north to Sacramento from UCLA at five a.m., six lanes of traffic were backed up. It looked like they were going to work; personally, I'm not sure how you stand living there.

189

Going to Los Angeles, I stopped in Nevada for the night and thought I would give a few pennies to a casino. I logged in a penny machine, one cent with twenty lines. Before I made my next move, I saw a button on my right that I though made the machine go around, so I pushed on it. On the screen was three lines, five times, three lines, five times, and three lines; the machine went nuts, and I was wondering what I did to cause all the ruckus? On the button, it read, "Maximum bet," that I pushed by mistake. I never told the casino that I made a mistake, and it gave me about $240 in pennies, and it took almost a half hour.

Coming back to Casper, I stopped at a red light, and going by on the green light was a police car with Dumbass Nevada painted on the side. I was wondering where I was at.

Then I made a trip to Tacoma, Washington, and then later in the same summer, I went to Branson, Missouri, for a USS Comstock LSD 19 reunion. I'm not sure why all the ship reunions don't take place there. Music is good for the soul. At one time, Nevada had a lot of entertainment, but they found out all you need is a slot machine in a telephone booth to make money. What is a telephone booth? We even had music when we ate breakfast form Denny Yeary and Gary Welch. The Ozark's Kirkwood Tour and Travel made arrangements for us the last times for the shows, etc. we stayed at the Stone Castle Hotel, and each one of us to the various shows and around town.

Doug Gabriel, behind my back, asked our leader if he had anyone that could come up on stage to help him out. Our leader gave him my name. so in the middle of his program, he came and got me out of the audience. He took

190

me up on the stage and dressed me up like Elvis. He sang "I'm in love, I'm all shook up," and at the proper time in the song, that was my part. I

impressed Doug so much with my shaking, etc., that he asked me if I had ever been on stage before, and he gave me a CD.

The worst rest stops that I encountered on the three trips were in Oklahoma. It looked to me like they built them with no faith in humanity at all. They were the only ones that I saw vandalized and dirty.

In Arkansas, I went in a restroom, and I turned the latch on the stall to lock, but the latch had been put on backward.

It was beautiful day, the day before we got a fair amount of snow. I pull the .22 rifle in the Jeep and drove about sixty miles from Casper to hunt rabbits. I made a lunch and stopped a small grocery store for a few extra things, which was odd. I drove off the main road onto a secondary road. On the way, I shot a rabbit, not far from the road, and when I got to my destination, I shot two more rabbits. The wind came up, and before I could get back to the Jeep, it must have been blowing sixty to seventy miles an hour. It occurred to me that I was in trouble, as the snow that had come down the day before was blowing horizontally. The Jeep was a four-wheel drive, but if you can't see where you're going, that doesn't help. It wasn't long and the Jeep wouldn't go any farther. Now I knew why I bought a few extra things to eat. During the night, a jackrabbit ran across the hood; that was how high the snow was pled around me. I was lucky I had a candle to light. I never wanted to run the engine of the car but save gas to eventually drive the Jeep back to Casper. The temperature was five below zero, and I was also afraid that the tail pipe was stopped up with snow, and that could cause carbon monoxide poisoning. I have, in the past, been accused of being a thinker.

At three a.m., I saw a truck turn around, and I turned on my lights, but they were covered with snow, and Edna was riding in the truck. When you are in a car like that, the bad part is when you have to go to the bathroom.

The next morning, I decided that I never wanted to spend another night in the Jeep, so I disobeyed the rules of getting stranded, about saying with the vehicle, and left the Jeep. After walking to the main road, I turned left because the wind was blowing in my face so hard. I should have turned right because a farmhouse was just around the bend of the road. A man and woman in a pickup stopped, and they took me back to the farmhouse. The truck that had turned around at three a.m. came to the farmhouse and took me home. I was embarrassed. It was the rescue truck, and it had a snowmobile, but he was uncertain that I was down that road so he never took it off. The next day, I asked Tom, Edna's son if he would take me back out and get the Jeep. He had a winch on the front of his truck because he was a big-game hunter. When we got to the Jeep, he tied the winch cable on and pulled me out of the ditch backward. I drove the Jeep beck to the house in Casper.

A few years later, I built a double car garage for a prime rib dinner, and that was all, to pay him back for coming after the Jeep.

He had one of the lumberyards (Sutherlands) bring a package deal of lumber, all in one load, of material to build it with. That was a good idea because you can use up a lot of time going after material. A contractor poured the footing and slab to build it on. The first day working in August, it was close to 100 degrees temperature. I never drank enough water and almost had a heat stroke trying to accomplish too much.

The business agent at the carpenter's hall called me up to a fire station to build from scratch, which I had never done before. Because the soil was bad under the footings, the first thing I had to do was lay out the building. I asked the superintendent if he would get me one corner that was at a ninety-degree angle with the transit, and I could do the rest. He did that and went back to the shed where the blueprint was located.

About ten a.m., the assistant business agent showed up after I had only been there a couple of hours. The boss was next to me, and he said, "Oh, I see you got Mickey. He doesn't wake up until ten." I could hardly believe that he said that about one of the carpenters from the carpenter hall. I knew that day I would get the oink slip (get fired) at quitting time or at least by Friday.

After the building was laid out, the next project was driving a stake where we wanted to drill a hole down to the bedrock and pour the concrete mixture. They had to be positioned under the footing.

The boss hired a couple of other carpenters, and we got the fire station built. He never did lay me off.

About a month ago, I got a natural gas bill for .38 cents, and it took a .44 cent stamp to send it in.

Because of Agent Orange that the United States sprayed in the foliage in Vietnam and the military men that were in the areas, it caused different kinds of diseases, and one of those was diabetes. I was in the navy, in an out of the coast and ports of call about five years. When I heard about the diabetes and Agent Orange, I went down to sign up. They told me that I had to prove that I went to shore I sent off for my record, and they never had anything in them that I ever went to shore. The only thing that I had was Vietnam money that I called my cab fare to the local bar. I saved a little money from each country that I entered. They wouldn't accept that, so I have to pay for my own medications, etc. it was seldom that when there was liberty call that I ever missed going to town. When I had duty, I would pay someone to stand in for me or do my duties.

After falling from the ladder on a construction job, I mentioned to the doctor that I was having a hard time hearing. He sent me to a doctor to have an examination. I went in a booth with a girl to have my audio exam, and afterward, she told me that I couldn't hear. She sent me to the doctor, and he
looked in both ears, confirmed that I couldn't hear and sent me home.

Three years later, I went back to the same doctor, and the new girl in the audio booth looked in my ears. She told me that she couldn't give me the audio exam until I had the doctor remove the wax. He removed wax out of both ears that was probably there since I played on the farm, and I went through eight years in the navy. The dark colored wax was about the size of a pencil. He told me that when I was there before that I never had wax in my ears. He said I never needed to have an audio exam and that I could go home. When I was in the navy, the ships that I was on had loose asbestos insulation flying around in the engine and pump rooms every time we had a major shipyard repair. I had to stand fire watch when a welder welded the pipes. The welding stinger or rod is covered with asbestos.

Then I worked about ten years in the construction trade, where asbestos insulation was used. One day, I got a letter from the carpenter union hall that told me there and have an x-ray to see if I had asbestoses. A month later, I got a letter that said I had asbestos in my lungs.

Because no one can sue the navy, where I got the disease, the attorney had to go after the different companies that were involved with asbestos. I filled out two pounds of paperwork and, over a period of twenty years, managed to receive about for thousand dollars.

I thought that I would try and get a medical condition card from the government to pay all my medical expenses. They sent me to a VA hospital for x-rays, and they couldn't see any problem with m y lungs.

I sensed that there was something wrong and sent a request for a read out of the payments from the attorney. He sent me information of what he had on the subject. About four months later, I received a letter that said the attorney was putting most of our money in his own private account. After he was sued, he filed for bankruptcy. He stole about seventeen million dollars and received a fifteen-year sentence. They said they couldn't find money, so we are out of luck. They gave my account to another attorney, and about every ten years, I get a paper to fill out. The last that I heard, the original attorney was appealing his sentence.

What I wanted from a local doctor was a second opinion about my lungs, and I would pay for it out of my own pocket. I passed all the tests that he gave me, and when he listened to my heart, he said that I should go to a heart specialist. I told ahead and make an appointment.

When I went to the heart doctor, he told me to lay up on the table for an examination. He took his right hand and made a spear out of his fingers. He shoved his spear down in my right hernia in my crotch and asked me, "Does it hurt?"

I almost died, the pain was so great, but I told him, "No, it didn't hurt."

He made an appointment for me to walk on the treadmill at the hospital. I walked on that until he got bored and shut off the machine.

It wasn't long after that, I had to have the right hernia operated on twice. What a heart doctor was doing down in my crotch. I'll except to say he damaged the inguinal hernia.

Because I have had only one accident when the police were called in 1955, that cost about $150, qualities me to give a few tips in defensive driving. I'm writing this book on 2011.

There was a certain amount of luck involved, and one of you had better be alert if a mistake is made.

Try to avoid the accident, no matter who was at fault. An insurance company canceled my insurance when I tried to get insurance in another state, after I left California to South Dakota. It never helped when I told them that I was lying on the couch when the accident happened.

When stopping at a stop sign and another car is behind you, put your brake on before you get to the stop sign or another cat to see if the other car slows down by looking in your rearview mirror. If they don't slow down, either get out of the way or be ready to put your brake on to avoid damaging the car in front of you.

Try and never stop on the street, making a left turn: either slow down, speed up, or go to the next block to turn.

On the trip, eat a moderate breakfast, and don't eat another thing until you get to your destination or motel room for the night. Going to sleep can kill you.

Always use the signal lights, instead of stop signs whenever possible. If you know the area, it is helpful. The driver ahead should always have the right to wait, when making a left turn at a signal light. I stopped the car a distance from the intersection, indicating for them to go ahead of no one is behind me and make their turn. If you are going to the right, you can usually turn anytime in most states, even if it is red.

If the light is green, that is when you should start checking to see what the other lanes of traffic are doing and if everybody is happy.

Move to other lanes slowly and never make any sudden maneuvers with your turn signal on.

Keep as far away from the trucks as you can get and stay out of their blind areas all the time. If you can't see their rearview mirror, they can't see you.

There was a man that drove out in front of an eighteen-wheeler with his girlfriend. What was she doing when he stopped and went out into traffic? Both of them were killed. What is the matter with being a back seat driver? It's not your sister, brother, mother, or ex-wife in the car. Instead of words, I use a short audio sound to warn of danger; it is much faster. They say we came from monkeys.

On a road with a possibility of running into a deer at night, I try and follow a safe distance behind an eighteen-wheeler, even if it means going slower, especially a two-lane road. We still have those in Wyoming.

Distractions of any kind could be a death sentence. There is always or usually the option of pulling off the road. The life you save could be your own.
If you don't have automatic locks on your car, lock all the doors when you get inside, especially of you are a woman and men are at risk also.

Stand on a corner and watch the cars going by the speed limit, and imagine being hit by one of them. Fasten your seat belt, no matter if you are on the interstate, highway, or downtown. One of the guys in our last driver's education class, for a reduction on our car insurance, said he never fastens his seat belt in town. If the truth was known, he probably never fastens his seat belt. If the car in front of you is turning right or left with his blinker on, I put my blinder on at the same time to warn or inform the person behind me. They turn right. I turn my blinker off, and go straight ahead. So far, no one has died.

If I know that I'm going to stop, I push my brake pedal down a few times to work the brake light, and so far, it had prevented anyone from saying they're sorry.

If you're drinking, it is a good idea to have all your car parts in working order. You don't want to give the police any excuse to pull you over.

Excessive speeding is asking for trouble, like "Come and get me." in the fifties, we could get away with radar. Use the speed control as much as possible, and set it at the speed limit.

Never drive beyond the white line because the rock you pick up and throw at the car behind you is not your car, but it could be your brother, sister, or mother's windshield. In cold climate, the rocks congregate beyond the white line from the winter weather and snowplow, etc.

When it is possible, watch the front wheel of any car in your vicinity. Believe it or not, a human brain is affecting the front wheel.

Back up only far enough as necessary from parking spaces, etc., and never park out in the parking lot waiting for your husband or wife, like a sore thumb. It is not natural; you could be run into.

The first colonoscopy that I had, the doctor must have run into a blockage when he got about eighteen inches inside or his mistress was waiting for him. He pulled the tool out. He cut off two polyps to send them to the lab. I thought that was easy, I'm not sure why I had shot. I was conscious the entire time.

Three years later on my second colonoscopy, I told them that I never needed a shot because in my mind, the first one was so easy. The second time, the doctor never spared anything but gave me the whole ball of wax, and I almost died. I told Edna afterward that I never received a shot, and she said she had never heard of a colonoscopy being given without a shot first. She had been a nurse. It is not the colonoscopy that gets you but the preparation. If your house doesn't have at least two bathrooms, I'm not sure how the preparation can be accomplished.

Several years, I played league pool in Casper, Wyoming, until about six years ago, and I beat the entire league players by one game, but the league wouldn't give me the honor. I quit playing the game, and by the standards that we had always played by, I won. It was confirmed by the powers that be.

The first pool hall I ever went into, I must have been twelve years old, and women weren't allowed to go inside. That was about 1950. They had more billiard tables (without holes) than anything else, and I never learned how to play that game.

It had been six years since I played on a team and was asked this year in 2011 to be one of the players. A couple of weeks ago, I won an eight-ball tournament (undefeated) playing some of the best players and got first place, winning $90. Just yesterday, I found out I have a cataract on one eye that needs removing.

When Tinney, Dad's brother, was killed in the underground mines in Missouri, Tinney's brother, Clifford, married Tinney's widow. We never did know if it was for love or money. Clifford was a good-looking man that the girls went crazy over. He had curly hair, etc. the marriage lasted his entire life. In downtown Casper, I made a wrong turn, and the police officer was at my window, asking for my driver's license, he saw another vehicle do a discretion of the law and told me to stay here. He said that he would be right back and kept my driver's license. After stopping the other driver and giving them a ticket, he drove back to my car and wrote me out a ticket. One night after we finished playing pool in a league, I'm not sure why I did it, but I never stopped completely at a 4x4 lighted stop sign, sober. The officer asked me if I saw the stop sign. I told him no, and I probably could count on two fingers the times that I have been stopped when they gave me a warning instead of a ticket.

After I hired a company to clean my wood burning stove's chimney, the man went up on the roof with five gallons of black tar. He smeared it all over the flashing and at the top of the chimney where the insert comes out of the brick. I was unhappy and I called the company to have the owner come over to the house. I wanted to talk to him. When he arrived, he said that he would have only smeared a little tar over there, and that made me mad, as the roof wasn't leaking.

First, I took pictures of it and took them to my lawyer that I had used several times in my real estate transactions. He told me to take my picture and find another attorney. The question that I had was, did he mean on this case or like "find another attorney." I have never been back to see him. I'm not sure why he was so riled up.

I went down to file a small claim document for almost three thousand dollars. On the claim form, it asked if I contacted the owner for reimbursement of the damages. After contacting him again, he paid for a reroofing job and to redo about three feet of brick on the chimney.

Mom was brought home in a car from town by one of her friends, and she noticed how easy it was to get out of the car with a handicap. She also noticed it had a For Sale sign in the window, and I bought it. I told a friend that I really made a mistake buying that car, as it uses oil. He told me to watch the oil and that it had only thirty thousand miles on it.

After outing ninety thousand miles on the car, a mechanic told me it needed the motor overhauled because the oil light was coming on when the motor was hot.

I put an advertisement in the newspaper to sell it for six hundred dollars in the bargain buggies ad and it runs. The body was made of metal, and they are given in demolition derbies. The first caller told me he would come by and look at it. The second caller, after I told him a couple of people said they would be by and look at it, told me he would buy it after getting off work. About an hour later, he called back to tell me his brother would be by and look at it. On the test run with me driving, it couldn't have run any better. The brother sent a picture sent a picture of the car with his cell phone and told his brother how nice it ran. With me driving, he never noticed the oil light that came on. At nine thirty that evening, the buyer came and gave me six hundred dollars without looking at the car. There is an old saying of "buyer, beware," and this was a classic example of that expression. Four men that worked at a coal mine bought the car to drive to work, and what I was told the second Buick that I couldn't kill; the other one was a 1950.

Chapter 20

PAUL

Paul never had much of a childhood. When he was about seven, he had to help Dad build the house in Laramie, Wyoming, and he felt the wrath of Dad more than any of the other siblings. He would get a migraine headache, and Dad told me years later that he thought Paul was trying to get out of work. When we moved down on the farm in 1942, he must have been twelve years old and did more of the farming than Dad because Dad was the preacher.

They did all the farming with horses and with the farm machinery related to that kind of farming.

After Paul graduated from high school, it looked like he was going to make a life on the farm, but they got into some kind of argument, and Dad told that the farm wasn't big enough for two men. He left the farm, and after a couple of jobs, one on a farm, the other in construction, he joined the United States Air Force. He put in twenty years in the air force and retired, but along the way, he married a Japanese woman. She had five children. She went back to japan after Paul got the children in the divorce. He was transferred to Scotland, married a young woman over there, and she had six children. One child was with another woman that he never married. His last marriage was with a Philippine woman, and they have one son. He told me he was a veteran of foreign women. Before he met the last one, we were going to Thermopolis, Wyoming. He looked over at me and said, "I have to find a woman with five kids," At the time, he had twelve children. In Tacoma,

204

Washington, my niece's husband asked me, "What is it with Paul and children?" I told him I never knew.

After getting out of the air force, he went to universities in Oklahoma and received a doctorate degree. He taught college classes in the State of Washington until he retired permanently. While living in Tacoma, he started a business, selling merchandise that was bought in Mexico.

He had his Lincoln up on two small ramps that you drive up on, and when he unhooked the transmission, it rolled backward. He never had any blocks behind the wheels, and the car crushed most of his ribs.

At the time, he was building sides on about a twenty-foot flatbed trailer, so Mom and I went to Tacoma to finish the trailer. There were two beds in the house. Mom slept in his bed, and I got the other one upstairs. At the time, there must have been six other people in the house. In a couple of days, when I got the trailer finished, we went back to Casper, Wyoming.

The next thing that I was told was the wife from Scotland became overly angry and busted up almost everything Paul had in the house. With the broken ribs, Paul couldn't prevent her wrath from taking place.

She fell in love with a man that owned a secondhand store, and she married him after she was divorced from Paul. In the settlement, she got the business, and it went downhill after she acquired it. The children continued living with Paul.

If you can imagine this, go ahead. Paul put a flat roof mad out of glass on the back of the house in Tacoma,

Washington, where it is no stranger to rain. From the beginning, if he ever got the daily leakage stopped all at one time, I couldn't tell you when it was. He was repairing the roof and fell through the plate glass after he retired from the college. I drove from Casper to help him finish fixing the roof. When I worked in the glass panels, I would put a board to walk on over the glass. It must have not been enough of an example because it wasn't long after I got back to Casper that he drove a nail into the glass and it shattered. He went through the roof and hit his head on the corner of the rock fireplace below. It was an accident waiting to happen, which was much worse than falling through the first time. He was in good shape physically until after these two falls, and he has had trouble ever since with his back, etc.

When he retired from teaching, his house went up for sale, and after he sold it, I went to Tacoma to help him move what he had left in a moving container that he had rented to take to Oklahoma City, Oklahoma.

He had married his last wife before he moved, and about five days after she had their son, my mother passed away in 1994. That was his thirteenth child.

Helen drove the Lincoln. The three of us, Matthew, Paul, and I, drove the truck with a fifth wheel trailer they lived in until he had a house built by a contractor in Oklahoma City.

I believe it was in Idaho that I noticed the pin that connected the truck to the trailer had lost the carter key, and it was almost out of its bracket. If that happened, the trailer would have disconnected from the truck.

In Rock Springs, Wyoming, we burned the bearing out of one of the dual wheels on one side of the trailer. Because of a snowstorm behind us, I probably drove faster than we should have went, when Paul went to sleep. I had a plane reservation to bring me back to Casper the day after we arrived in Oklahoma City.

We removed the tire, and from Rock Springs to their new hometown, we pulled the trailer with only one tore on one side. I was told that was a dangerous thing to do, but it worked for us, so sometimes, it's good to be lucky.

We were out of propane, and Paul sent me inside to have the bottle filled. The attendant took the bottle, carried it through a half door, and out a side door. After a while, Paul came in and asked me what I was doing.

"I'm waiting for the propane," I told him.

And Paul said, "It's out in back, maybe I was supposed to follow the guy."

He had a new house built that just missed two tornados, and with thirteen children, it was not very compatible for guests, but to each his own. The only good room for a guest bedroom was made it into computer room.

Chapter 21

SIS

After sis married Merlyn, she joined the Catholic church bodily but not in spirit. Eventually, Merlyn shied away from the Catholic faith, and his children suggested that. When he died, he was buried in a Catholic cemetery in Cuba City, Wisconsin, where he lived all his life. He drove a cab in Dubuque, Illinois, and worked in the mines when Sis met him. A good share of his life, he lived on social security disability.

Merlyn's parents gave them a corner of their land, and it had a very small house on it. You might say that Sis jumped from the frying pan into the fire.

At first, they used an outhouse, and the water was drawn from a well in the backyard. She did the wash by hand or eventually a coin Laundromat in Cuba City, Wisconsin. It wasn't until just before Merlyn died that the finally bought a washer and drier after about fifty years of marriage.

Because they were Catholic at the time, they had three girls living in the little house with not much more than three rooms, and later, she had two sons, when they lived in a basement, to build the rest of the house on later.

The problem was they had to pay cash for everything, which was Merlyn's idea of living his entire life.

They put a top floor on the concrete walls, with building paper on it, to keep out the rain, the same way Dad did it in Laramie, Wyoming. I'm not sure how long they lived in the basement, but it could have been years. I was told there were very few walls that had been put in the basement for privacy matters. Either Dad or Mom told me that even the bathroom never had any walls put around it.

I'm not sure at the time if Merlyn or Sis realized how much the children at school tantalized their children, with all of them living in the basement. Cuba City is a small town, and as they say, everybody knows everybody. Karla, the daughter, told me she dreaded to go school, just a few years before she died of an enlarged heart.

I was there in 1965 and slept with Dad in a bedroom in the unfinished house, when I took a thirty-day leave in the navy. Dad was working on the house then, and they were still living in the basement. They were married in 1949, so either they were living in the small house or basement, with three to five children, for sixteen years at least. After I went to the fiftieth wedding anniversary, it got me to thinking about Merlyn's life and if he deserved all the praise that he got. I'm going to leave that up to the family, but they should take a good honest look at it.

In 1963 or '64, Sis was going to the Cuba City dump to take their garbage, and she had a daughter and son in the car. She had a wreck, and her head got out of the door that came open prematurely but was never fixed. A metal highway guide post hit her neck, and it fractured five vertebrae.

Today, she doesn't walk very well, and part of the time, she uses a walker or wheelchair. Her condition today can be traced back to the car accident.

We have a good time on the telephone. I have told her more than once she was a good straight man, and she can ask some of the strangest questions. It leaves me with a good response that leaves us booth laughing.

When my niece had her house built, she built a three-bedroom, three-bath apartment on the side of her house. She said it was for Merlyn and Sis when they got old. A few days ago, I found out a religious organization had something to do with it being built so big. The cultist lived in the house several years, and they were the cause of her divorce from her first husband. In the divorce settlement, she received a lot of money. Sis sold the two houses in Cuba City after Merlyn died and received about $150,000 for both of them. Sis moved to the apartment and lived there about two years.

After going to the hospital, she went to a nursing home to recuperate. While there, her daughter hot footed it to Cuba City, Wisconsin, and made arrangements for the eventuality. She never said one word to Sis, and it turned out that she wanted to be buried next to Karla in a plot that Sis bought for her husband, who never wanted it in Colorado Springs.

When she brought her home from the nursing home, she took her over to her house to live in one room and bath without asking Sis about anything. She tried to make do with a microwave oven and washed her dishes in the lavatory in the bathroom. If it's not cruelty to one's parent, evidently, I don't know it when I see it. I n Cuba City, while living with her parents, Karla seldom went on a date with a guy. Not long after they moved to Colorado Springs, she met and married a nuclear scientist. With an enlarged heart, she died not long after they returned from South Korea; he went there for a job assignment. I was told that a person with enlarged heart shouldn't fly in an airplane.

She was only married about two months so my niece told Sis that she had to pay for all the funeral expenses because she wasn't married long enough. Sis bought the two plots, the most expensive casket, and paid for the catered food after the funeral service.

Sis had already paid for an automatic chair lift to her apartment that my niece should have gotten Medicare to pay for through a doctor's prescription.

My niece never liked the wheelchair that I gave them, which my mother used for years. It was light but efficient. She gave it to the Goodwill Store. Sis bought a battery-powered wheelchair, like the one you see in the television ads, when the lady said, "And I never paid a dime out of my pocket." It had a hydraulic lift that was attached to the back of my niece's car.

They can't possibly get in the house, so recently, Sis bought another push wheelchair that didn't have a brake for the person sitting in the chair nor side metal wheels. It was just for someone to push with her sitting in it. I never knew they even made one like that. Two years ago, I bought a wheelchair form Casper when I went to get her that I rented.

The car that they brought with them form Wisconsin developed a transmission problem, and I told them to get it fixed. They bought another car that was hardly ever used, and they gave it to her son from an affair after Karla died.

I never knew this until last summer that her grandson bought an expensive car, and before Karla died, she asked Sis to sign the papers with him. He was living in the apartment rent-free, and he quit making the payments on the car, so Sis paid the car off to save her good credit. He stole a television and moved back to live with his brother in Oregon with the car that was paid for. I told Sis that she should not have paid it off but let the bank repossess it. At her age, she didn't need good credit anymore.

This is only one way that you can get rid of about $130,000 in less than two years and the inheritance that should have went to the rest of her children.

Sis asked me one time what I thought of Merlyn's casket. I told her I thought it was too expensive, but it never registered. She did the same thing at Karla's funeral with a picture of her put on the headstone.

After my mother's funeral, I made ham and cheese sandwiches.

Finally, after being told that she wasn't a good mother, she did what she should have done a long time ago and moved into a subsidized government apartment complex in Milledgeville, Illinois. Her cat had died, which she wasn't allowed to replace, and shortly, she was going to get another cat. I believe now she is the happiest that she has ever been in her entire life. She just had an eightieth birthday party, with most of her relatives present.

Chapter 22

DAD

Dad would ask me sometimes, "Don't you like the way I operate?"

I'm not sure what he would have done if I had told him that I never liked the way he operated.

The other siblings never got as many kisses as I did. Every time he passed gas, he told me, "There's a kiss for you, Mick."

When he quit the railroad twice and we almost starved on the farm when he was preaching, looking back, it showed me he never cared for anybody but himself.

When Paul and Dad greeted each other, they would say, "Hello, stud," and the other, "Hi, stud."

In the book, he is mentioned a lot, so I will write about after he retired as a union carpenter.

He went to Miller, Missouri, and built an addition onto the farmhouse of five acres but never stayed there very long. I never did see it. One of his daughters lived with him under questionable circumstances until she left with a man that took her to Texas for a short trip. She told me one time that she couldn't understand why she never got pregnant.

Dad bought a lot in Springfield, Missouri, and tore a brick building down for the siding. He built a three-bedroom house. He laid the used brick, standing on his truck bed, as he moved it around the house.

When I went for a visit, there was black soot on everything in the house. He had been burning his garbage in a wood stove in the garage, and he thought all the smoke was going out the garage door opening.

He decided to sell the house and he bought an Airstream trailer. He sold the house contract for deed, and somehow in the transaction, the deed was given to the new buyers in their name.

Sis and Merlyn drove from Wisconsin to help him move his personal things to the trailer. Merlyn was carrying canned food that Sis had given him, from the house to the trailer, when Dad stopped him. He said that he had to take it back, as he sold them with the house.

After the new owners saw that the deed was already in their name, they stopped paying the mortgage, and it took him a long time to get the house back in his name. In the meantime, they were getting free rent.

He met a woman at the senior center and moved in with her. After he got his house back, they moved back in Dad's house, as it had more space. The greatest compliment that he ever gave me was when he said I could build a house on two saw horses. It would be possible because using math, a person can figure out the length of rafters, windows, door headers, etc.

About thirty miles from Branson, Missouri, he bought a lot, an eight-foot-wide trailer, and boat with a boat trailer. He had a dock on the Arkansas River, where he never had to take the boat out of the water. Branson was in its infancy in the entertainment business, and he sold it all for $3,000.

When Sis and Merlyn was visiting Dad, he had Clifford's (brother) trailer parked in the front of his house for sale. He had died of cancer. Merlyn asked Dad from Cuba City what he received for the trailer. Don't told him nothing. He said that he advertised it for$1,500 in the newspaper, and a man came by in a nice suit with a truck. He asked Dad if he could take the trailer for a test drive to see how it pulled, and that was the last time he saw it.

Both parents weren't the touchy-feely kind, and I only remember one time that Dad told me that he loved me on the last trip that he came to Casper after eighty years. I never said anything. I never heard Mom say those words.

One day, Dad and his girlfriend were playing cards. He had a heart attacked and died. One of Dad's girlfriends of long ago supposedly had two children in Casper in the fifties, and one of them inherited everything that he owned. He was buried in the older Joplin, Missouri, cemetery with a few of his other relatives, and he was also born in Joplin.

When I was driving down to the funeral, I received a ticket for speeding in Clinton, Missouri, number 4 for the year. Driving back to Casper, I received number 5 tickets in Dodge City, Kansas. I asked the highway patrol officer, as nice as I could, if he would give me a warning. He asked me why. I told him that he was writing my fifth ticket for the year. It could have been worse; I had a loaded .22 rifle in the trunk. The cop wasn't impressed and kept writing my ticket. In Casper, I had to hire my favorite attorney to get me off, and the judge or attorney found an error on the Clinton, Missouri, ticket, and it saved my driver's license. At the time, the speed limit on secondary roads was 55 miles an hour with 65 posted on the interstate highways.

Chapter 23

MOTHER

Mom had polio when she was three years old, and after years of working as a cook in restaurants, with only one good leg, she developed rheumatoid arthritis. She had to quit work and live on social security disability.

While I was in the navy, she got married the second time to northern California, where Murphy saw a few of his old drinking buddies, and he fell off the wagon as they say. When they arrived back in Rapid City, it wasn't long before he got drunk and put a shotgun shell in my .410 to blow the little toe of his foot. The police took my gun, and Mom got a divorce. Murphy had a stroke, probably from a blood clot from the shotgun blast, and Mom told the VA Hospital she could take care of him. She discovered that he was too much for her to take care of. They were married the second time; he was a World War II veteran. He couldn't say, "I do." He grunted; that was close enough. Mom asked the VA hospital in Hot Springs, South Dakota, to come and get him.

We went to Hot Springs several times for a visit, and while there, I went swimming in the hot mineral swimming pool, as I had done since I was fourteen.

Remarrying Murphy was the best thing that she ever did because of the money they gave her when she had to go to a nursing home herself, but it only helped. It took the money from the VA, Social Security, and money that I received form my real-estate business to keep her there. I had to pay out so much money for four years that I had to quit remodeling a house and let it set empty.

When Murphy was in Hot Springs, I was going to the carpenter vocational school in Rapid City. Murphy had another stroke that killed him, and he is buried in the VA Cemetery between Rapid City and Sturgis, South Dakota.

From another lady Mom knew, she was told that there was a doctor in Mexicali, Mexico, that had a cure for rheumatoid arthritis. She made a couple of trips down there. He gave her a pill that caused migraine headaches almost weekly. On one of her trips, a man took her crutches away from her, and he wanted money to give them back. She told him she never needed them and he gave them back anyway.

She found out that a man in Casper was buying the pills in Mexico and reselling them here. She had run out of pills and called him up to find out if he was home. He was home and she said that she couldn't go anyplace, so I went over to get the pills. And he never had any clothes on, sitting in a wheelchair, when I went inside.

After she quit taking the pills, she never had another migraine headache.

After she sold the house to the government in Rapid City she came over to Casper and bought a house. She offered the people about five thousand dollars less than what they asked, and they accepted it, but we didn't know it at the time they were angry. They took the cat box out of the house, and the cats went to the bathroom all over until closing, about thirty days later. The cat odor lasted for years.

We thought that the moving van would pick up the furniture and deliver it in a timely manner, but it was several days until they showed up. We thought all her furniture was stolen.

When I graduated from the carpenter class in Rapid City, Mom wanted me to enroll in an Agriculture Business Vocational School. I was the top student in the carpenter class, but evidently, she never had any faith that I could do the work.

Every Friday night, I was going from work and eating supper at her house. She had written almost every chamber of commerce in every town in Arkansas to have a realtor send her a list of farms that were for sale. After we finished eating supper, I had to pick one out. The carpenter job was the first time in my life that I had ever made any money, and she wanted me to move to a farm. We took time we got back, she said that she decided she was too old to live on a farm.

In one of the restaurants, on the way back, I was sitting at a table, and Mom had gone to the rest room. When she came out on crutches, she had about five feet of toilet paper dragging behind her. I was embarrassed to say the least, so I asked her, "What is that?" She said the restroom was dirty.

As Mom got older, she was less able to do the things she once did. The first thing that we had to do was hire someone to help with the cleaning of the house. They started stealing everything that wasn't nailed down. I was living in the other side of town in a trailer house. They took bedding, a Rogers Silverware set that she received when she got married, towels, sheets, etc.

Two years later, we had to hire someone to live in the house and take care of her full time for about four years. They had to put a brace on her leg that the polio damaged dress her, and fix all the meals. On Saturday night, I helped her get into a chair that lowered into the bathtub. Then I put her to bed. We always let the girl that took care of her have Saturday off.

She had kept a diary up to this time, but she was scared the girls would read it, so she quit. We never needed a real qualified person, so we never had to pay all that much of a salary. Over the four years, we probably hired at least twenty-five different girls.

About the time that we started hiring help, I started buying real estate, and on a moment's notice, I could go over to her house to assume taking care of her.

One girl went after a package of Camel cigarettes and never came back.

Most of the time, I would get the groceries on Saturday, but if they needed something, the grocery store was within walking distance. Mom told one of the girls to go get something from Safeway, and she told her that she got caught shoplifting in there and was barred. She must have been putting the money in her pocket and stole the needed items to supplement her income.

When a girl never worked out, Mom would fire them, and I would have to go live in her house until we ran advertisement to hire someone else.

We finally got a person that stayed a couple of years, and my brother Paul was visiting with us. She brought something to drink over to the table, and Paul said, "Boy, you're ugly."

Up to that time or since, I had never heard a person say that in the face of anyone before. He never realized how hard it was to keep hired help on the wages that we could afford.

Mom's profession resent her, telling them how to do anything in the kitchen. A lot of them would put something on the stove and go watch TV. That always irritated Mom the most.

It was common practice for some of them to take their boyfriends down in the basement to show them how large it was.

Mom saw an advertisement in the newspaper that they had a program to help poor people pay part, if not all, their natural gas bill. I took all the necessary paperwork to them, and we got to talking about her income. They told me that she never qualified. Because it was money going to another person as wages, but living in the same house, common sense told me that they should have taken it off her income.

In Casper, for a long time, we never had any eye surgeon that removed cataracts, so every year, a group would drive up here from Salt Lake City, Utah. For ten years, they would send my mother a letter for her to make an appointment that they would be in Casper on such and such a day. It was all a waste of time and money. Telling this to Edna, she said, "Why didn't you know it, at the time, how slow a cataract grows?"

How should I have known that? I just barely finished high school.

The girl that stayed the longest went on vacation, and went to live with Mom until she got back. I noticed every night it took her longer to walk from the front room chair to her bed. One night, I didn't think she was going to make the trip. The next morning, I was a little hesitant to put her brace on, but she insisted. After I put it on, she couldn't walk a step. Mom said, "You better go find a nursing home for me." I came back to the house, put her in the wheelchair, took her out to the car, and drove her to her new home for about four years. I found out when it was too late, that wasn't the way I should have done it. A doctor should have had her committed to the nursing home, so I never got one dime of help financially from the government. When she was put in a room, the head nurse called me into the office and had me sign a paper that I wouldn't bother the government for her nursing home cost. The reason for this is the government doesn't pay as much for a person's care as an individual must pay.

Another mistake we made was I never got her house in my name thirty months before she went into the nursing home. I paid all her bills, which was about fifty thousand dollars over the four-year period, just from my real estate alone. The way I understood it, welfare would have paid her bill, but we would have had to sign the house over to them. If I sell the house, I'm not sure how the capital gains was going to play out, but you can be it wasn't going to be pretty. A little over the last month that she lived, she was on welfare when she died. At eleven minutes until two a.m., I got a call that she had died, and it was on the eleventh of November. Mom was born in the year 1911. With the arrangements that I had to do, it was three days later that I went to retrieve her personal things. I was told her stuff was through that door over there. I went out the door, and it had snowed during the night. Her stuff had about six inches of snow on it.

People spend too much money on funerals, and I believe it is money thrown away. I got one of the cheapest caskets, and after the funeral, I made ham and cheese sandwiches, which you could have as many of them as you wanted.

Marriages could fall under this same category. I just read in the newspaper that Diana and Charles of England spent five million, and we all know what happened to that love nest. Prince Rainer and Grace Kelly, ten million, and so far the record that I know of is twenty-nine million. I hope they are still together. There are too many people starving to death in the world for this nonsense.

Chapter 24

ELIJAH'S DILEMMA

Thursday evening, at a Chinese restaurant, my fortune cookie never had anything in it. I complained to the waitress, and she brought me another one. It sad needed to talk to someone. My favorite song is sung by Frank Sinatra, "I Did It My Way," but looking back, my life has been spared too many times to think that I have been by myself without God when I was a sinner or saint.

When I wrote the book *The Way, the Truth, and the Life*, there was a book before that, but after the editor was finished with it, I never recognized my own book. It's under my desk. Then after several bouts with soul-searching, it occurred to me that my biblical name is Elijah the prophet of Malachi 4:5. "Behold, I will send you Elijah the prophet before the coming of the great and dreadful day of the Lord."

Do you remember the dove that I said was white that went in my mouth? In these verses, I find an explanation for that. St. Matthew 13:16 says, "But blessed are your eyes, for they see: and your ears, for they hear." Revelation 2:7 says, "He that hath an ear let him hear what the Spirit saith unto the churches; To him that overcometh will I give to eat of the tree of life, which is in the midst of the paradise of God. " Revelation 2:17 says, "He that hath an ear, let him hear what the Spirit (Holy Ghost) saith unto the churches; (mankind) To him that manna, and will give him a white stone, (dove) and in the stone a new name written, which no man knoweth saving (except) he that receiveth it."

St. John 6:31-34 deals with manna which is changed to bread: "My father giveth you the true bread from heaven. For the bread of God is he which cometh down from heaven, and giveth life unto the world. (He, is the Holy Ghost <Spirit> or bread form heaven) Then said they unto him, Lord, evermore give us this bread.

The Elijah of the Old Testament has nothing to do with the Elijah for this dispensation. That is the dilemma that I'm writing about in this chapter. The KJB of 1611 tells us that John the Baptist was Elijah. How could this be, when Elijah is to come before the coming of the great and dreadful day of the Lord or at the end-time? Wasn't John alive at the time of 'Jesus? How can we say than that John the Baptist was Elijah? It was the disciples that said Elijah was John the Baptist in St. Matthew 17:13, but the eleventh verse says, "Jesus answered and said unto them, Elijah truly shall first come, and restore all things." In St. John 1:21, it says, "And they asked him (john the Baptist) What then? Art thou Elijah? And he saith, I am not. Art thou that prophet? And he answered, No."

Without the parables being explained, would it be fair for God to bring on the end-time, especially without anyone knowing about the salvation plan?

The preachers want to believe that John the Baptist was Elijah for some reason. It could ne they say the Bible has no error, which is wrong in the first place. It is misleading because
of the parables. The preachers understand it literally, and that is a mistake or the world has a different Bible all together.

Then there is the group that says Elijah came at the time of the transfiguration, which meets all the requirement for Malachi 4:5. I'm not sure how anybody can consider that to be true. When he appeared with Moses, it was the Elijah that appears at the end-time, as it says, "At the great and dreadful day of the Lord."

The third nonfiction book that I wrote, the name of it was *Elijah, the Last Prophet*. I might have sold twenty books before the publisher ended our relationship. When an author is from a Missouri farm, a carpenter, born at the time, without a suitable place to live, with scars on their body, and received the Holy Ghost the same way Jesus did, but without the water. Someone should tie it all together and I might have sold more books.

"How is it that he eateth and drinketh with publicans and sinners? When Jesus heard it, he saith unto them, they that are whole (believe they are whole) have no need of the physician, (God nor Jesus) but they that are sick: (Those that know they need a savior) I came (not) to call the righteous, but sinners to repentance" (St. Mark 2:16-17).

Yes, they were self-published books. I was in a hurry to get the message of salvation out to the public but never considered the hardheadedness of the preachers and religious organizations with a different doctrine, Bibles, man-made ceremonies, Etc. I read where 80 percent of people wouldn't even consider that their parents were wrong. Now we have 20
percent to work with. Jesus left the ninety-nine and went after the one; is that telling us something?

St. John 8:44 says, "Ye are of your father the devil, and the lusts of your father ye will do. He was a murderer from the beginning, and abode not in the truth, because there is no truth in him. When he speaketh a lie, he speaketh of his own: for he is a liar, and the father of it. And because I (Jesus) tell you the truth, ye believe me not. They never believed Jesus, what chance do you think I have?"

Only God could tell you what is meant about what will happen exactly at judgement day, but the 'gospel of Matthew had verses in regard to rewards. It could be better than a kick in the pants. Whatever the rewards are, I couldn't tell you.

St. Matthew 10:40 says. "He that receieveth you receiveth me, and he that receiveth me receiveth him that sent me. He that receieveth a prophet in the name of a prophet shat receive a prophet's reward; and he that receiveth a righteous man in the name if a righteous reward. And whosoever shall give to drink unto one of these little ones cup of cold water only in the name of a disciple, verily I say to unto you, he shall in no wise lose his reward."

Explaining the parables or allegory writing of the King James Bible of 1611, mainly St. John, Matthew, and Mark, that is what my job is.

Twice the Tree of Life has been mentioned. The only explanation when given it is the same morning I saw an angel, at midnight, a sensation was felt in my body; it must have been the Tree of Life.

"He that hath an ear, let him hear what the Spirit saith unto the churches; To him that over cometh (from the false doctrine) will I give to eat of the tree of life, which is in the midst of the paradise of God."(Revelation 2:7)

"And the Lord God said, Behold the man is become as one of us, to know good and evil: and now, lest he put forth his hand, and take also of the 'tree of life', and eat, and live forever."(Genesis 3:22)

"So he drove out the man; and he placed at the east of the garden of Eden cher-u-bim, and a flaming sword which turned every way, to keep the way of the tree of life." (Genesis 3:24)

Jesus knew it would be difficult. That is why my livelihood has been taken care of, other than through any churches or religious organization.

CPSIA information can be obtained
at www.ICGtesting.com
Printed in the USA
BVHW041452180520
579860BV00011B/899